Better Homes & Gardens.

Hometown

FAVORITES

Delicious down-home recipes

Volume 9

Meredith Consumer Marketing
Des Moines, Iowa

Better Homes & Gardens.

Hometown Favorites

MEREDITH CONSUMER MARKETING
Consumer Marketing Product Director: Heather Sorensen
Consumer Marketing Product Manager: Wendy Merical
Consumer Marketing Billing/Renewal Manager: Tami Beachem
Business Manager: Diane Umland
Senior Production Manager: Al Rodruck

WATERBURY PUBLICATIONS, INC.
Editorial Director: Lisa Kingsley
Associate Editor: Tricia Bergman
Creative Director: Ken Carlson
Associate Design Director: Doug Samuelson
Production Assistant: Mindy Samuelson
Contributing Copy Editors: Gretchen Kauffman, Peg Smith
Contributing Indexer: Mary Williams

BETTER HOMES AND GARDENS® MAGAZINE
Editor in Chief: Stephen Orr
Senior Deputy Editor: Nancy Wall Hopkins

MEREDITH NATIONAL MEDIA GROUP
President: Tom Harty

MEREDITH CORPORATION
Chairman and Chief Executive Officer: Stephen M. Lacy

In Memoriam: E.T. Meredith III (1933–2003)

TEST KITCHEN

Our seal assures you that every recipe in *Hometown Favorites* has been tested in the Better Homes and Gardens. Test Kitchen. This means that each recipe is practical and reliable, and it meets our high standards of taste appeal. We guarantee your satisfaction with this book for as long as you own it.

All of us at Meredith Consumer Marketing are dedicated to providing you with information and ideas to enhance your home. We welcome your comments and suggestions. Write to us at: Meredith Consumer Marketing, 1716 Locust St, Des Moines, IA 50309-3023.

Pictured on front cover:
Italian Roast Beef Slider Melts, page 77
Photography by Carson Downing

Contents

CHAPTER 1
Appetizers, 4

CHAPTER 2
Poultry, 28

CHAPTER 3
Meat, 68

CHAPTER 4
Seafood, 106

CHAPTER 5
Sides, 132

CHAPTER 6
Desserts, 160

INDEX, 188

Appetizers

Of all of the elements of a perfect party, yummy food tops the list! These dips, spreads, and snacks will guarantee your next gathering is a great one.

6   Chicken and Eggplant Stuffed Shells

8   Salmon and Cheese Stuffed Mushrooms

9   Ham Balls in Barbecue Sauce

11   Korean Beef Lettuce Wraps

12   Fried Pickled Peppers with Ginger Aïoli

13   Picadillo Poppers

14   Stuffed Fresh Sweet Peppers

16   Classic Nachos

17   Baby Potatoes Roasted in Salt

18   Sriracha Deviled Eggs

19   Bacon-Filled Medjool Dates

20   Prosciutto-Basil Cheese Balls

21   Baked Tomato-Mozzarella Spread

22   Pizza Dip

23   Fire-Roasted Tomato Salsa

24   Barbecue-Spiced Roasted Chickpeas

25   Cheesy Snack Mix

26   Pink Rhubarb Lemonade

27   Sangria

14

16

26

Chicken and Eggplant Stuffed Shells

These shells—crispy on the outside and stuffed with a savory combination of chicken and eggplant flavored with garlic and fennel—are a healthier at-home take on the favorite restaurant appetizer of toasted ravioli.

PREP 30 minutes
BAKE 18 minutes at 375°F

12 servings	ingredients	24 servings
	Olive oil nonstick cooking spray	
12	dried jumbo shell macaroni	24
⅓ cup	chopped onion	⅔ cup
⅓ cup	chopped red sweet pepper	⅔ cup
1 Tbsp.	olive oil	2 Tbsp.
¾ cup	chopped eggplant	1½ cups
2	cloves garlic, minced	4
¼ tsp.	fennel seeds, crushed	½ tsp.
½ cup	chopped cooked chicken breast	1 cup
½ cup	crumbled feta cheese	1 cup
1	egg, lightly beaten	2
⅓ cup	seasoned fine dry bread crumbs	⅔ cups
¾ cup	marinara sauce, warmed	1½ cups
⅓ cup	fresh basil, thinly sliced	⅔ cups

1. Preheat oven to 375°F. Line a 9×13-inch baking pan with foil; coat foil with cooking spray. Cook macaroni shells according to package directions; drain. Rinse with cold water; drain again. Invert shells on paper towels to dry.

2. Meanwhile, for filling, in a skillet cook onion and sweet pepper in hot olive oil over medium heat 3 minutes, stirring occasionally. Add eggplant, garlic, and fennel seeds. Cook 3 to 4 minutes more or until vegetables are tender, stirring occasionally. Remove from heat; stir in chicken and feta cheese.

3. Pour egg into a bowl. Pour bread crumbs into another bowl. Dip the outside of each pasta shell in the egg, allowing excess to drip off. Dip coated shell in bread crumbs, turning to coat. Lightly spray outsides of shells with cooking spray. Place shells in the prepared pan, crumb sides down. Spoon chicken filling into shells.

4. Bake 18 to 20 minutes or until heated through and bread crumbs are lightly browned. Transfer shells to a platter. Spoon marinara sauce over shells; sprinkle with fresh basil.

FOR 24 SERVINGS Use two 9×13-inch baking pans.

PER SERVING *104 cal., 4 g fat (1 g sat. fat), 26 mg chol., 198 mg sodium, 12 g carb., 1 g fiber, 6 g pro.*

Salmon and Cheese Stuffed Mushrooms

Not a fan of fish? Try the bacon-stuffed variation below. Or do half and half for variety.

PREP 15 minutes
BAKE 17 minutes at 425°F
STAND 5 minutes

20 servings	ingredients	40 servings
20 large	cremini or button mushrooms	40 large
4 oz.	thinly sliced smoked salmon (lox-style), chopped	8 oz.
one 5.2-oz. pkg.	semisoft cheese with fines herbes	two 5.2-oz. pkg.
	Chopped green onions or fresh snipped parsley (optional)	

1. Preheat oven to 425°F. Lightly grease a 15×10-inch baking pan. Wipe mushrooms with a paper towel. Remove stems from mushrooms; discard or reserve for another use. Place tops, stem sides up, on prepared pan.

2. Divide smoked salmon among mushrooms, pressing down lightly. Top each with about 1½ tsp. semisoft cheese.

3. Bake 17 to 20 minutes or until mushrooms are tender. Let stand 5 minutes before serving. If desired, sprinkle with onions or parsley.

FOR 40 SERVINGS Use two 15×10-inch baking pans.

TO MAKE AHEAD Prepare as directed through Step 2. Cover and refrigerate up to 24 hours. Before serving, continue with Step 3.

PER SERVING *44 cal., 3 g fat (2 g sat. fat), 10 mg chol., 103 mg sodium, 1 g carb., 0 g fiber, 3 g pro.*

BACON-STUFFED MUSHROOMS Prepare as directed, except omit salmon. For 20 servings, cook 8 slices of bacon until crisp; drain on paper towels and crumble. For 40 servings, Cook 16 slices of bacon. Stir together semisoft cheese and crumbled bacon; spoon into mushrooms. Continue as directed.

Ham Balls in Barbecue Sauce

Salty, savory, and sweet, these saucy meatballs are quick to mix up. With more than one set of hands involved in the rolling, they're fast to finish, too. If you like, keep them warm in a slow cooker set on low during the party.

1. Preheat oven to 350°F. Lightly grease a 9×13-inch baking dish. In a large bowl combine the first five ingredients (through pepper); stir in half the mustard. Add ground ham and pork; mix well. Shape into 24 balls, using about 3 Tbsp. for each. Arrange ham balls in the prepared baking dish.

2. For sauce, in a bowl stir together the remaining mustard and remaining ingredients; pour over ham balls. Bake 25 minutes or until done (160°F).

FOR 48 SERVINGS Use two 9×13-inch baking dishes. Shape meat mixture into 48 balls.

PER SERVING *92 cal., 3 g fat (1 g sat. fat), 34 mg chol., 204 mg sodium, 10 g carb., 0 g fiber, 6 g pro.*

PREP 20 minutes
BAKE 25 minutes at 350°F

24 servings	ingredients	48 servings
2	eggs, lightly beaten	4
1½ cups	soft bread crumbs	3 cups
½ cup	finely chopped onion	1 cup
2 Tbsp.	milk	¼ cup
¼ tsp.	black pepper	½ tsp.
2 tsp.	dry mustard	4 tsp.
12 oz.	ground cooked ham	24 oz.
12 oz.	ground pork or beef	24 oz.
¾ cup	packed brown sugar	1½ cups
½ cup	ketchup	1 cup
2 Tbsp.	vinegar	¼ cup

Korean Beef Lettuce Wraps

Use either butter lettuce or iceberg lettuce as the shell for these wraps. Butter lettuce is tender and pliable while iceberg is crisp and crunchy.

1. In an extra-large skillet cook beef over medium-high heat until browned. Stir in soy sauce, sriracha sauce, and sesame oil. Stir in broccoli slaw. Cook and stir over medium heat 2 to 3 minutes or just until slaw is wilted.

2. Spoon beef mixture onto lettuce leaves. Top with red sweet pepper and, if desired, peanuts and/or green onions and additional sriracha sauce. Serve with lime wedges.

PER SERVING *185 cal., 7 g fat (2 g sat. fat), 53 mg chol., 567 mg sodium, 9 g carb., 3 g fiber, 21 g pro.*

START TO FINISH 20 minutes

4 servings	ingredients	8 servings
12 oz.	extra-lean ground beef	24 oz.
3 Tbsp.	reduced-sodium soy sauce	6 Tbsp.
1 Tbsp.	sriracha sauce	2 Tbsp.
2 tsp.	toasted sesame oil	4 tsp.
one 12-oz. pkg.	shredded broccoli slaw	two 12-oz. pkg.
8	butter lettuce or iceberg lettuce leaves	16
½ cup	red sweet pepper, cut into strips	1 cup
	Chopped peanuts and/or sliced green onions (optional)	
	Lime wedges	

Fried Pickled Peppers with Ginger Aïoli

A bit like a popper without the stuffing, these crunchy and fiery bites get a cooldown from a dipping sauce of mayonnaise, ginger, and lime.

PREP 25 minutes
FRY 2 minutes per batch

6 servings	ingredients	12 servings
⅓ cup	mayonnaise	⅔ cup
2 tsp.	grated fresh ginger	4 tsp.
1½ tsp.	fresh lime juice	1 Tbsp.
⅛ tsp.	kosher salt	¼ tsp.
¼ cup	olive oil	½ cup
1 Tbsp.	minced green onion	2 Tbsp.
3 cups	whole or halved jalapeño peppers* or pepperoncini salad peppers, drained	6 cups
¾ cup	buttermilk or sour milk**	1½ cups
1 cup	all-purpose flour	2 cups
1 cup	yellow cornmeal	2 cups
1 Tbsp.	black pepper	2 Tbsp.
	Peanut or vegetable oil for deep-fat frying	

1. For Ginger Aïoli, in a bowl whisk together mayonnaise, ginger, lime juice, and salt. Gradually whisk in oil. Stir in green onion. Cover and chill until serving.

2. Preheat oven to 200°F. Line a baking sheet or a wire cooling rack with paper towels. In a bowl combine jalapeño peppers and buttermilk. In a plastic bag combine flour, cornmeal, and black pepper.

3. In a Dutch oven or large saucepan heat 2 inches of oil to 375°F.

4. Place a handful of peppers in flour mixture and shake to coat. Remove peppers, shaking off excess flour mixture. Using a slotted spoon, add peppers to hot oil. Fry 2 to 3 minutes or until crisp and golden. Transfer with slotted spoon to wire rack. Keep warm in oven while frying remaining peppers. Serve with Ginger Aïoli.

FOR 12 SERVINGS Use two baking sheets.

*TIP Chile peppers contain oils that can irritate your skin and eyes. Wear plastic or rubber gloves when working with them.

**TIP To make ¾ cup sour milk, place 2 tsp. lemon juice or vinegar in a glass measuring cup. Add enough milk to equal ¾ cup liquid; stir. Let stand 5 minutes before using. For 1½ cups sour milk, use 4 tsp. lemon juice or vinegar and add milk to equal 1½ cups liquid.

PER SERVING *428 cal., 28 g fat (4 g sat. fat), 6 mg chol., 817 mg sodium, 39 g carb., 3 g fiber, 6 g pro.*

Picadillo Poppers

Picadillo is a sweet-savory dish made of ground beef, pork, or veal; onion and/or garlic; tomato; and golden raisins that's popular in many Spanish-speaking countries. It's eaten with rice, on bread, or stuffed into peppers—sweet or hot.

1. For filling, in a large skillet cook ground beef and onion over medium-high heat until meat is browned and onion is tender. Drain off fat. Stir in the next five ingredients (through sherry).

2. Cut a lengthwise slit in one side of each jalapeño to create a pocket (do not cut pepper in half). Cut a small slit crosswise on both ends of the long slit, making an L-shape opening. Leave stem intact and use a small spoon to remove seeds and membrane. Spoon filling into peppers.

3. Place filled peppers, slit sides up, in a greased grill basket or grilling pan. Grill, covered, over medium heat 8 to 12 minutes or until peppers are crisp-tender and filling is heated through. If desired, top with additional cheese.

PER SERVING *74 cal., 4 g fat (2 g sat. fat), 11 mg chol., 107 mg sodium, 7 g carb., 1 g fiber, 4 g pro.*

PREP 45 minutes
GRILL 8 minutes

24 servings	ingredients	48 servings
8 oz.	lean ground beef	16 oz.
⅓ cup	chopped onion	⅔ cup
one 8.8-oz. pouch	cooked Spanish-style rice	two 8.8-oz. pouches
1 cup	shredded Monterey Jack cheese	2 cups
½ cup	golden raisins	1 cup
½ cup	sliced pimiento-stuffed green olives	1 cup
1 to 2 Tbsp.	dry sherry or lime juice	2 to 4 Tbsp.
24	fresh plump jalapeño peppers (tip, page 12)	48

Stuffed Fresh Sweet Peppers

These fresh, light, and crunchy mini peppers stuffed with an avocado-cream cheese filling make a refreshing addition to an appetizer buffet.

START TO FINISH 45 minutes

15 servings	ingredients	30 servings
15	miniature sweet peppers	30
1	medium avocado, seeded, peeled, and cut up	2
4 oz.	cream cheese, softened	8 oz.
¼ cup	basil pesto	½ cup
2 tsp.	lemon juice	4 tsp.
	Thinly sliced fresh basil (optional)	

1. Cut miniature sweet peppers in half lengthwise. Remove seeds and membranes.

2. Meanwhile, for filling, in a food processor combine the next four ingredients (through lemon juice). Spoon filling into pepper halves.

3. Serve immediately or cover loosely and chill up to 4 hours. If desired, sprinkle with thinly sliced basil just before serving.

PER SERVING *69 cal., 6 g fat (2 g sat. fat), 10 mg chol., 66 mg sodium, 3 g carb., 1 g fiber, 1 g pro.*

Classic Nachos

For game day or any day, this pile of crispy chips loaded with beef, beans, salsa, cheese, and a whole host of fresh toppings hits the spot.

PREP 20 minutes
BAKE 20 minutes at 350°F

8 servings	ingredients	16 servings
5 cups	tortilla chips	10 cups
1 lb.	ground beef	2 lb.
one 15-oz. can	black beans or pinto beans, rinsed and drained	two 15-oz. cans
1 cup	chunky salsa	2 cups
1½ cups	shredded cheddar cheese, Colby and Monterey Jack cheese, or Mexican-style four-cheese blend	3 cups
	Toppings, such as thinly sliced green onions, snipped fresh cilantro, seeded and sliced fresh jalapeños (tip, page 12), sour cream, and/or chunky salsa (optional)	

1. Preheat oven to 350°F. Arrange half the tortilla chips on an 11- to 12-inch oven-going pan.

2. In a large skillet cook ground beef over medium heat until browned; drain off fat.

3. Stir black beans and the 1 cup salsa into beef. Spoon half the beef mixture over chips. Sprinkle with half the cheese. Bake 10 minutes or until cheese is melted; remove from oven. Top with remaining chips, beef mixture, and cheese. Bake 10 minutes or until is cheese melted. Add toppings.

FOR 16 SERVINGS In Step 1, use two 11- to 12-inch oven-going pans. In Step 2, divide the beans and 2 cups salsa between the two pans.

PER SERVING *368 cal., 21 g fat (8 g sat. fat), 61 mg chol., 638 mg sodium, 26 g carb., 5 g fiber, 23 g pro.*

Baby Potatoes Roasted in Salt

Baking these baby potatoes in a salt crust doesn't actually make them salty. It does draw the moisture out of the surface of the potatoes, which gives them an extra-crisp crust with a tender, buttery interior.

1. Preheat oven to 425°F. In a bowl combine half the olive oil and the garlic; brush on the bottom and sides of a 9×13-inch baking dish. Sprinkle rosemary in dish. Place potatoes in a single layer on rosemary.

2. In a bowl combine salt and flour. Gradually stir in water until combined. Spoon salt mixture evenly over potatoes, pressing firmly.

3. Roast 45 to 50 minutes or until potatoes are tender. Cool in pan on a wire rack 5 minutes. Using a thin metal spatula, loosen the salt crust from side of dish. Carefully invert potatoes and salt crust onto a large serving platter. Drizzle potatoes with the remaining olive oil and sprinkle with pepper.

FOR 30 SERVINGS Use two 9×13-inch baking dishes.

PER SERVING *105 cal., 4 g fat (1 g sat. fat), 0 mg chol., 1,163 mg sodium, 17 g carb., 2 g fiber, 2 g pro.*

PREP 25 minutes
ROAST 45 minutes at 425°F
COOL 5 minutes

15 servings	ingredients	30 servings
¼ cup	olive oil	½ cup
4	cloves garlic, minced	8
3 Tbsp.	snipped fresh rosemary	6 Tbsp.
3 lb.	small new potatoes and/or fingerling potatoes	6 lb.
3 cups	kosher salt	6 cups
¼ cup	all-purpose flour	½ cup
½ cup	water	1 cup
	Freshly ground black pepper	

Sriracha Deviled Eggs

Spicy Asian chili sauce gives this classic appetizer a modern twist. If you like things fiery, drizzle the finished eggs with additional sriracha sauce.

PREP 25 minutes
STAND 15 minutes

16 servings	ingredients	32 servings
8	eggs	16
⅓ cup	mayonnaise	⅔ cup
1 Tbsp.	sriracha sauce	2 Tbsp.
1 Tbsp.	fresh lime juice	2 Tbsp.
¼ tsp.	salt	½ tsp.
¼ tsp.	ground ginger	½ tsp.
	Pickled sliced ginger, fresh cilantro leaves, and/or chopped green onions (optional)	

1. Place eggs in a single layer in a saucepan. Add enough cold water to cover eggs by at least 1 inch. Bring to a rapid boil over high heat. Remove from heat, cover, and let stand 15 minutes; drain. Run cold water over eggs or place in ice water until cool enough to handle; drain and peel. Halve eggs and remove yolks. Set whites aside.

2. In a bowl stir together egg yolks and the next five ingredients (through ginger). Using a rounded teaspoon, stuff egg white halves with yolk mixture. (Or place yolk mixture in a large resealable plastic bag; snip off one corner of the bag. Pipe onto each egg white half.) Cover and chill up to 24 hours. If desired, top with pickled ginger, cilantro, and chopped green onions. Drizzle with additional sriracha sauce.

PER SERVING *68 cal., 6 g fat (1 g sat. fat), 95 mg chol., 120 mg sodium, 0 g carb., 0 g fiber, 3 g pro.*

Bacon-Filled Medjool Dates

These stuffed dates hit on every level. You'll taste crunchy nuts, tangy melty cheese, smoky and salty bacon—and of course the sweetness of the dates— all in one bite. Just be sure to cool slightly before serving. The sugary dates get very hot in the oven!

1. Preheat oven to 375°F. In a large skillet cook bacon over medium heat until crisp. Transfer bacon to paper towels to drain; crumble bacon. In a bowl stir together the bacon, almonds, and cheese.

2. Slit one side of each date and remove pit. Spoon about 1 Tbsp. of the bacon filling into each date; press date to shape around filling (filling will be exposed). Arrange dates, filling sides up, in an 8×8-inch baking pan.

3. Bake 12 to 15 minutes or until heated through and cheese is lightly browned; cool slightly. Before serving, drizzle warm dates with honey and sprinkle with thyme.

FOR 24 SERVINGS Use a 9×13-inch baking pan.

*TIP To toast nuts, seeds, or coconut, preheat oven to 350°F. Spread them in a shallow baking pan. Bake 5 to 10 minutes or until lightly browned, shaking pan once or twice. Or toast small amounts in a dry skillet over medium heat for 2 minutes or until fragrant and golden, stirring frequently.

TO MAKE AHEAD Prepare as directed through Step 2. Cover and refrigerate up to 2 days. Continue as directed, baking 15 to 18 minutes.

PER SERVING *112 cal., 3 g fat (1 g sat. fat), 4 mg chol., 79 mg sodium, 21 g carb., 2 g fiber, 2 g pro.*

PREP 25 minutes
BAKE 12 minutes at 375°F

12 servings	ingredients	24 servings
3 slices	bacon	6 slices
¼ cup	whole almonds or pecan halves, toasted* and chopped	½ cup
¼ cup	finely shredded Manchego or Parmesan cheese	½ cup
12	unpitted whole Medjool dates	24
1½ Tbsp.	honey	3 Tbsp.
½ tsp.	snipped fresh thyme	1 tsp.

Prosciutto-Basil Cheese Balls

What's better than your very own personal-size cheese ball? These two-bite beauties will delight your guests.

1. In a large bowl place cream cheese, Fontina cheese, and butter; let stand at room temperature 30 minutes. Add milk. Beat on medium until light and fluffy. Stir in green onion, basil, and prosciutto. Cover and chill 4 to 24 hours.

2. For each cheese ball, form 2 tbsp. cheese mixture into a ball. Roll balls in pine nuts; let stand 15 minutes. Serve with sliced pears, crackers, and/or flatbread.

PER SERVING *224 cal., 22 g fat (8 g sat. fat), 47 mg chol., 286 mg sodium, 3 g carb., 0 g fiber, 7 g pro.*

PREP 35 minutes
STAND 45 minutes
CHILL 4 hours

12 servings	ingredients	24 servings
one 8-oz. pkg.	cream cheese	two 8-oz. pkg.
4 oz.	Fontina cheese, finely shredded	8 oz.
¼ cup	butter	½ cup
1 Tbsp.	milk	2 Tbsp.
2 Tbsp.	thinly sliced green onion	¼ cup
2 Tbsp.	snipped fresh basil	¼ cup
2 oz.	prosciutto, chopped	4 oz.
1 cup	pine nuts, toasted and chopped (tip, page 19)	2 cups
	Sliced pears, crackers, and/or flatbread	

Baked Tomato-Mozzarella Spread

If you need an appetizer for a crowd—a big crowd—this is the thing to make. Just stir together the sauce, sausage, and pesto—and press the mozzarella balls into the surface. Bake until bubbly, then dig in!

1. Preheat oven to 350°F. Coat an 8×8-inch baking dish with cooking spray. In a bowl stir together pasta sauce, sausage, and pesto; pour into prepared baking dish. Press mozzarella balls into the sauce.

2. Bake 25 to 30 minutes or until bubbly and mozzarella is softened. Drizzle with olive oil and top with fresh basil leaves. Serve with toasted baguette slices.

FOR 84 SERVINGS Use a 3-qt. baking dish.

TO MAKE AHEAD DIRECTIONS Prepare as directed through Step 1. Cover and refrigerate up to 24 hours. To serve, continue as directed in Step 2.

PER SERVING *100 cal., 8 g fat (2 g sat. fat), 19 mg chol., 248 mg sodium, 3 g carb., 0 g fiber, 5 g pro.*

PREP 15 minutes
BAKE 25 minutes at 350°F

42 servings	ingredients	84 servings
	Nonstick cooking spray	
one 24-oz. jar	garlic pasta sauce	two 24-oz. jars
1 lb.	bulk mild Italian sausage, cooked and crumbled	2 lb.
¼ cup	pesto	½ cup
8 oz.	bite-size fresh mozzarella balls or cubes	16 oz.
	Olive oil	
	Fresh basil leaves	
	Toasted baguette slices	

Pizza Dip

Served with warm wedges of bread for dipping, this cream cheese-based dip flavored with tomatoes, Italian cheese, pepperoni, mushrooms, and green peppers is essentially a deconstructed pizza.

1. Preheat oven to 350°F. In a blender combine the first four ingredients (through onion powder). Cover and blend until well mixed.

2. In a bowl combine cream cheese, half the Italian cheese, and the sour cream. Spread cream cheese mixture in a 9-inch pie plate. Pour tomato mixture over cream cheese layer. Sprinkle with remaining Italian cheese, pepperoni, mushrooms, and sweet pepper.

3. Bake 25 minutes or until bubbly and lightly browned. Serve with bread wedges.

FOR 64 SERVINGS Use two 9-inch pie plates.

PER SERVING *100 cal., 6 g fat (3 g sat. fat), 17 mg chol., 238 mg sodium, 7 g carb., 0 g fiber, 3 g pro.*

PREP 20 minutes
BAKE 25 minutes at 350°F

32 servings	ingredients	64 servings
one 14.5-oz. can	diced tomatoes, drained	two 14.5-oz. cans
2 tsp.	dried Italian seasoning	4 tsp.
¼ tsp.	garlic salt	½ tsp.
¼ tsp.	onion powder	½ tsp.
one 8-oz. pkg.	cream cheese, softened	two 8-oz. pkg.
1 cup	finely shredded Italian cheese blend	2 cups
½ cup	sour cream	1 cup
one 5-oz. pkg.	sliced pepperoni, halved	two 5-oz. pkg.
⅓ cup	chopped fresh mushrooms	⅔ cup
⅓ cup	chopped green sweet pepper	⅔ cup
	Italian bread shell, such as Boboli, warmed and cut into wedges	

Fire-Roasted Tomato Salsa

Grilling the vegetables gives them a wonderful smoky flavor and beautiful charred bits.

1. Place the garlic cloves on a square of heavy foil. Drizzle with oil. Bring up edges of foil around the garlic cloves to enclose.

2. Grill 8 of the tomatoes, the jalapeños, and one onion half, covered, directly over medium-high heat for 6 minutes or until tomatoes and peppers are blackened and blistered and onion is charred, turning once. Add garlic foil packet the last 3 minutes of grilling. Remove from grill and let cool. Stem and, if desired, seed jalapeños.

3. Meanwhile, finely chop the remaining onion half and remaining tomatoes. Set aside.

4. Place grilled tomatoes, onion, jalapeños, and garlic with oil in a blender. Cover and blend until nearly smooth. Transfer to a bowl; add the chopped tomatoes, finely chopped onion, cilantro, lime juice, and salt; toss to combine. Season to taste with additional lime juice and salt.

FOR 16 SERVINGS In Step 2, grill 16 of the tomatoes.

PER SERVING *17 cal., 0 g fat, 0 mg chol., 126 mg sodium, 3 g carb., 1 g fiber, 1 g pro.*

PREP 30 minutes
GRILL 6 minutes

8 servings	ingredients	16 servings
3	cloves garlic, peeled	6
1 tsp.	olive oil	2 tsp.
10	roma tomatoes, cored	20
3	jalapeño peppers (tip, page 12)	6
1	medium yellow onion, peeled and halved	2
3 Tbsp.	snipped fresh cilantro	⅓ cup
¼ cup	fresh lime juice	½ cup
1 tsp.	kosher salt	2 tsp.

Barbecue-Spiced Roasted Chickpeas

Italians love crunchy roasted chickpeas as a natural, high-protein snack. This recipe gives them a decidedly American flavor.

PREP 5 minutes
ROAST 30 minutes at 450°F

12 servings	ingredients	24 servings
two 15-oz. cans	no-salt-added garbanzo beans (chickpeas), rinsed and drained	four 15-oz. cans
¼ cup	olive oil	½ cup
1 tsp.	barbecue spice	2 tsp.
1 tsp.	paprika	2 tsp.
1 tsp.	chili powder	2 tsp.
¼ tsp.	garlic salt	½ tsp.
¼ tsp.	celery salt	½ tsp.
¼ tsp.	onion powder	½ tsp.

1. Preheat oven to 450°F. In a medium bowl combine all ingredients. Spread in an even layer in a 15×10-inch baking pan.

2. Roast 30 minutes or until browned and crisp, stirring once. Cool completely.

FOR 24 SERVINGS Use two 15×10-inch baking pans.

PER SERVING *101 cal., 5 g fat (1 g sat. fat), 0 mg chol., 122 mg sodium, 10 g carb., 3 g fiber, 4 g pro.*

Cheesy Snack Mix

You won't be able to stop at just one (small) handful of this crunchy mix. Cheesy, garlicky, savory, and smoky, it's absolutely addictive!

1. Preheat oven to 300°F. In a 15×10-inch baking pan combine cereal, shoestring potatoes, breadsticks, cheese crackers, and, if desired, almonds.

2. In a saucepan combine butter and salad dressing. Heat over low heat until butter is melted. Stir in cheese and garlic powder. Drizzle butter mixture over cereal mixture; toss gently to coat.

3. Bake 30 minutes, stirring twice. Spread snack mix on a large sheet of foil; let cool.

FOR 36 SERVINGS Use two 15×10-inch baking pans.

PER SERVING *128 cal., 6 g fat (3 g sat. fat), 10 mg chol., 238 mg sodium, 16 g carb., 1 g fiber, 3 g pro.*

PREP 15 minutes
BAKE 30 minutes at 300°F
STAND 1 hour

18 servings	ingredients	36 servings
4 cups	crispy corn and rice cereal	8 cups
one 1.75-oz. can	shoestring potatoes	two 1.75-oz. cans
2 cups	crisp breadsticks, broken into 2-inch pieces	4 cups
2 cups	bite-size cheese crackers	4 cups
one 6-oz. can	smoke-flavored whole almonds (optional)	two 6-oz. cans
¼ cup	butter or margarine	½ cup
3 Tbsp.	bottled clear Italian salad dressing	⅓ cup
¼ cup	grated Parmesan cheese	½ cup
¼ tsp.	garlic powder	½ tsp.

Pink Rhubarb Lemonade

This pretty-in-pink drink is so refreshing and a lovely choice for a spring or summer party.

1. In a large saucepan combine rhubarb and the water. Bring to boiling; reduce heat. Simmer, covered, 5 minutes. Remove from heat; cool slightly.

2. Strain rhubarb mixture through a sieve, lightly pressing to remove all the juice. Discard pulp. Add sugar and lemonade concentrate to rhubarb juice, stirring until sugar is dissolved. Cover and chill 2 to 24 hours.

3. In a punch bowl or large pitcher combine rhubarb mixture and lemon-lime beverage. Serve over ice. If desired, add mint, lemon slices, and/or rhubarb pieces.

PER SERVING *169 cal., 0 g fat, 0 mg chol., 29 mg sodium, 44 g carb., 0 g fiber, 0 g pro.*

PREP 20 minutes
CHILL 2 hours

8 servings	ingredients	16 servings
5 cups	fresh rhubarb, cut into ½-inch pieces, or frozen unsweetened sliced rhubarb	10 cups
2½ cups	water	5 cups
¾ cup	sugar	1½ cups
half a 12-oz. can	frozen pink lemonade concentrate, thawed	one 12-oz. can
one 1-liter bottle	lemon-lime carbonated beverage, chilled	two 1-liter bottles
	Ice cubes	
	Fresh mint leaves, lemon slices, and/or rhubarb pieces (optional)	

Sangria

The longer the wine, juice, brandy, and fruit chill and mingle in the refrigerator, the more flavorful the sangria will be.

1. In a large pitcher combine wine, orange juice, and brandy. If desired, sweeten to taste with agave nectar. If desired, add orange slices, lime slices, strawberries, and/or mango wedges. Cover and chill 3 hours or up to 24 hours.

2. Just before serving, add lemon-lime beverage; stir gently. Serve in glasses over ice. If desired, add mint.

PER SERVING *127 cal., 0 g fat, 0 mg chol., 9 mg sodium, 10 g carb., 0 g fiber, 0 g pro.*

PREP 5 minutes
CHILL 3 hours

8 servings	ingredients	16 servings
1 bottle	dry red wine	2 bottles
1 cup	orange juice	2 cups
¼ cup	brandy	½ cup
	Agave nectar or sugar; orange slices, halved; lime slices, halved; strawberries, halved; and/or mango wedges (optional)	
one 12-oz. can	lemon-lime carbonated beverage	two 12-oz. cans
	Fresh mint leaves (optional)	

CHAPTER 2

Poultry

Chicken and turkey are budget-conscious and mild in taste—which makes them adaptable to all kinds of flavors and preparations. Pick a few favorites here.

30 Creamy Chicken Enchiladas

31 Chicken Paillard Salad

32 Baked Curried Chicken with Cauliflower

33 Chicken Caesar Lasagna

35 Chicken and Broccoli Stir-Fry

36 Chicken Marsala Skillet

38 Chicken Fajitas in a Flash

39 Curried Chicken Salad

40 Italian Roasted Chicken and Vegetable Toss

43 Mexican Corn-Chicken Casserole

44 Peanut Chicken Satay Stir-Fry

45 Warm Brussels Sprouts Salad with Chicken

46 Greek Chicken and Pita Casserole

48 Greek Chicken Kabobs

49 Chicken Alfredo Cauliflower Rice Bake

50 Coconut-Curry Noodle Bowl

51 Honey-Sriracha Grilled Chicken Thighs

52 Nacho Chicken Drummettes

53 Butter Beans, Italian Sausage, and Chard

55 Chicken and Spinach Phyllo Bake

56 Rosemary and Ravioli Chicken Soup

59 Chicken Tortilla Soup

61 Sweet-Spicy Barbecue Chicken Sliders

62 Buffalo Chicken Rolls

64 Ham, Cheese, and Turkey Stromboli

65 Overgrown Garden Turkey Melt

67 Tarragon-Blue Cheese Turkey Patties

38

49

61

Creamy Chicken Enchiladas

These yummy chicken enchiladas are not a quick fix, but they are well worth the effort—and they bake for a little more than an hour, so you can clean up and sit down to eat with a clean kitchen. They're healthy, too—with only 270 calories and 10 grams of fat per serving.

PREP 50 minutes
BAKE 1 hour 5 minutes at 350°F
STAND 5 minutes

6 servings	ingredients	12 servings
8 oz.	skinless, boneless chicken breast halves	16 oz.
half a 10-oz. pkg.	frozen chopped spinach, thawed and well drained	one 10-oz. pkg.
¼ cup	thinly sliced green onions	½ cup
one 8-oz. carton	light sour cream	two 8-oz. cartons
one 4-oz. can	diced green chile peppers, drained	two 4-oz. cans
½ cup	milk	1 cup
¼ cup	plain yogurt	½ cup
2 Tbsp.	all-purpose flour	¼ cup
¼ tsp.	salt	½ tsp.
¼ tsp.	ground cumin	½ tsp.
six 7-inch	flour tortillas	twelve 7-inch
⅓ cup	shredded Monterey Jack or cheddar cheese	⅔ cup
	Fresh cilantro sprigs (optional)	
	Salsa (optional)	

1. Preheat oven to 350°F. In a large covered saucepan cook chicken in enough boiling water to cover for 12 to 14 minutes or until done (165°F); drain. Shred chicken using two forks.

2. In a bowl combine shredded chicken, spinach, and green onions. For sauce, in another bowl combine next seven ingredients (through cumin).

3. For filling, combine chicken mixture and half the sauce. Spoon filling just below centers of tortillas; roll up tortillas. Place, seam sides down, in an 8×8-inch baking dish. Spoon remaining sauce over tortillas.

4. Bake, covered, 65 to 70 minutes or until heated through. Sprinkle with cheese. Let stand 5 minutes before serving. If desired, top with cilantro and/or additional green onions and serve with salsa.

FOR 12 SERVINGS Use a 9×13-inch baking dish.

TO MAKE AHEAD Prepare as directed through Step 3, except do not spoon remaining sauce over tortillas. Cover dish and remaining sauce; chill 2 to 24 hours. Continue as directed.

PER SERVING *270 cal., 10 g fat (5 g sat. fat), 49 mg chol., 518 mg sodium, 26 g carb., 2 g fiber, 17 g pro.*

Chicken Paillard Salad

This light and refreshing combination of grilled chicken, tart and juicy grapefruit, creamy avocado, peppery arugula, baby spinach, and crunchy fennel in a citrus-champagne vinaigrette is a welcome meal on a warm summer night.

1. Using the flat side of a meat mallet, flatten chicken between two pieces of plastic wrap to ¼- to ½-inch thickness.

2. Lightly grease a panini griddle or indoor electric grill with oil. Heat over medium heat or according to manufacturer's directions. Add chicken; close lid and cook 4 minutes or until done (165°F). Slice chicken and place on dinner plates.

3. Meanwhile, for the vinaigrette, in a small bowl whisk together the next six ingredients (through pepper). Arrange arugula, spinach, grapefruit, avocado, and fennel on plates. Drizzle with vinaigrette. Serve with chicken paillard.

PER SERVING *314 cal., 11 g fat (2 g sat. fat), 82 mg chol., 271 mg sodium, 20 g carb., 6 g fiber, 35 g pro.*

START TO FINISH 20 minutes

4 servings	ingredients	8 servings
four 5-oz.	skinless, boneless chicken breast halves	eight 5-oz.
	Olive oil	
2 Tbsp.	grapefruit juice	¼ cup
1 Tbsp.	champagne vinegar	2 Tbsp.
1 Tbsp.	olive oil	2 Tbsp.
¼ tsp.	salt	½ tsp.
¼ tsp.	black pepper	½ tsp.
3 cups	arugula	6 cups
2 cups	shredded fresh baby spinach	4 cups
2	pink grapefruit, peeled and sliced	4
1	medium avocado, halved, seeded, peeled, and sliced	2
¾ cup	thinly sliced fennel	1½ cups
	Freshly ground black pepper (optional)	

Baked Curried Chicken with Cauliflower

It takes just 20 minutes to put together the ingredients for this flavorful one-dish meal. Put it in the oven and walk away while it fills your house with the wonderful aroma of curry and garlic.

PREP 20 minutes
BAKE 50 minutes at 375°F

6 servings	ingredients	12 servings
¼ cup	honey	½ cup
¼ cup	Dijon mustard	½ cup
2 Tbsp.	olive oil	¼ cup
1 Tbsp.	curry powder	2 Tbsp.
3	cloves garlic, minced	6
¼ tsp.	crushed red pepper	½ tsp.
six 6-oz.	skinless, boneless chicken breast halves	twelve 6-oz.
2 cups	cauliflower florets	4 cups
1	large sweet potato, peeled and cut into 1-inch pieces	2
1	large red sweet pepper, cut into bite-size strips	2
2 cups	hot cooked brown rice	4 cups
	Sliced green onions (optional)	

1. Preheat oven to 375°F. For honey-mustard, in a small bowl combine the first six ingredients (through crushed red pepper).

2. Arrange chicken in a 9×13-inch baking dish; brush with half the honey-mustard sauce. Add cauliflower, sweet potato, and sweet pepper; drizzle with remaining sauce.

3. Bake, covered, 25 minutes. Bake, uncovered, 25 minutes more or until done (165°F) and sweet potatoes are tender. Serve chicken and vegetables over rice and drizzle with cooking liquid. If desired, top with green onions and additional crushed red pepper.

FOR 12 SERVINGS Use two 9×13-inch baking dishes.

PER SERVING *429 cal., 10 g fat (2 g sat. fat), 124 mg chol., 353 mg sodium, 42 g carb., 5 g fiber, 42 g pro.*

Chicken Caesar Lasagna

Creamy, white-sauced lasagna and healthful eating are not mutually exclusive. This family-friendly dish is built with whole wheat lasagna noodles, light Alfredo sauce, chicken breast, chopped spinach, and roasted red sweet peppers.

1. Preheat oven to 325°F. Lightly coat a 9×13-inch baking dish with cooking spray. Cook lasagna noodles according to package directions; drain. Rinse with cold water; drain again. Meanwhile, in a bowl combine Alfredo sauce, lemon juice, and black pepper. Stir in chicken, spinach, and roasted peppers.

2. Arrange three noodles in the prepared baking dish. Top with one-third of the chicken mixture. Repeat layers twice.

3. Bake, covered, 45 to 55 minutes or until heated. Sprinkle with cheese. Bake, uncovered, 5 minutes more or until cheese is melted. Let stand 15 minutes before serving. If desired, top with tomatoes.

FOR 18 SERVINGS Use two 9×13-inch baking pans.

PER SERVING *268 cal., 10 g fat (6 g sat. fat), 68 mg chol., 557 mg sodium, 20 g carb., 2 g fiber, 24 g pro.*

PREP 35 minutes
BAKE 50 minutes at 325°F
STAND 15 minutes

9 servings	ingredients	18 servings
	Nonstick cooking spray	
9	dried whole wheat or regular lasagna noodles	18
two 10-oz. containers	refrigerated light Alfredo pasta sauce	four 10-oz. containers
3 Tbsp.	lemon juice	6 Tbsp.
½ tsp.	cracked black pepper	1 tsp.
3 cups	chopped cooked chicken breast	6 cups
one 10-oz. pkg.	frozen chopped spinach, thawed and squeezed dry	two 10-oz. pkg.
1 cup	roasted red sweet peppers, chopped	2 cups
¾ cup	shredded Italian cheese blend	1½ cups
	Cherry or grape tomatoes, halved (optional)	

Chicken and Broccoli Stir-Fry

Skip the expensive, unhealthy take-out! This veggie-packed dish is ready in just 30 minutes from start to finish. Serve it with hot oolong tea and chopsticks for a restaurant-style dining experience.

1. For sauce, in a small bowl stir together the first six ingredients (through sesame oil).

2. Cut florets from broccoli stems and separate into small pieces. Cut broccoli stems crosswise into ¼-inch slices.

3. In a large skillet or wok heat half the vegetable oil over medium-high heat. Add broccoli stems; cook and stir 1 minute. Add broccoli florets and sweet pepper; cook and stir 3 to 4 minutes or until vegetables are crisp-tender. Remove from skillet.

4. Add remaining vegetable oil to hot skillet. Add chicken; cook and stir 2 to 3 minutes or until no longer pink. Push chicken from center of skillet. Stir sauce; pour into center of skillet. Cook and stir until thickened and bubbly. Return vegetables to skillet; cook and stir 1 minute more or until heated through.

5. If desired, sprinkle stir-fry with toasted sesame seeds. Serve with hot cooked rice and, if desired, serve with additional hoisin sauce.

*TIP Toast sesame seeds in a dry skillet over medium heat 2 minutes or until fragrant and golden, stirring frequently.

PER SERVING *353 cal., 10 g fat (3 g sat. fat), 49 mg chol., 640 mg sodium, 34 g carb., 6 g fiber, 28 g pro.*

START TO FINISH 30 minutes

4 servings	ingredients	8 servings
½ cup	cold water	1 cup
2 Tbsp.	soy sauce	¼ cup
2 Tbsp.	hoisin sauce	¼ cup
2 tsp.	cornstarch	4 tsp.
1 tsp.	grated fresh ginger	2 tsp.
1 tsp.	toasted sesame oil	2 tsp.
1 lb.	broccoli	2 lb.
2 Tbsp.	vegetable oil	¼ cup
1	medium yellow sweet pepper, seeded and cut into thin strips	2
12 oz.	skinless, boneless chicken breast halves or thighs, cut into bite-size pieces	24 oz.
	Sesame seeds, toasted* (optional)	
2 cups	hot cooked rice or chow mein noodles	4 cups

Chicken Marsala Skillet

There is a reason this classic Italian dish remains in popular rotation. The combination of the crisp-crusted pan-fried chicken and meaty mushrooms luxuriating in an elegant, aromatic sauce spiked with Marsala wine is irresistible.

START TO FINISH 35 minutes

4 servings	ingredients	8 servings
¼ cup	all-purpose flour	½ cup
½ tsp.	dried thyme, crushed	1 tsp.
¼ tsp.	salt	½ tsp.
⅛ tsp.	black pepper	¼ tsp.
four 6- to 8-oz.	skinless, boneless chicken breast halves	eight 6- to 8-oz.
1 cup	chicken broth	2 cups
½ cup	dry Marsala wine	1 cup
3 Tbsp.	butter	6 Tbsp.
1 Tbsp.	olive oil	2 Tbsp.
2 cups	sliced fresh button or cremini mushrooms	4 cups
2 Tbsp.	finely chopped shallot	¼ cup
	Hot cooked pasta (optional)	
	Snipped fresh Italian parsley	

1. In a shallow dish stir together flour, thyme, salt, and pepper. Using the flat side of a meat mallet, flatten chicken between two pieces of plastic wrap to ¼-inch thickness. Dip chicken into flour mixture, turning to coat.

2. In a bowl whisk together any remaining flour mixture, the broth, and Marsala.

3. In an extra-large skillet heat 1 Tbsp. of the butter and the oil over medium-high heat. Add chicken; cook 4 to 6 minutes or until no longer pink, turning once. Transfer to a serving platter; cover and keep warm.

4. For sauce, add mushrooms and shallot to skillet; cook 6 to 8 minutes or until tender, stirring occasionally. Carefully add Marsala mixture. Cook and stir until slightly thickened and bubbly. Whisk in remaining butter until incorporated. Serve chicken with pasta (if desired) and sauce. Sprinkle with parsley.

FOR 8 SERVINGS In Step 3, use 2 Tbsp. of the butter.

PER SERVING *381 cal., 17 g fat (7 g sat. fat), 133 mg chol., 638 mg sodium, 11 g carb., 1 g fiber, 39 g pro.*

Chicken Fajitas in a Flash

This broiled sheet-pan version of chicken fajitas requires no messy sautéing—and it still turns out sizzling and delicious.

1. Preheat broiler. For sauce, in a medium bowl combine first seven ingredients (through salt). Remove ¼ cup of the sauce. Add chicken to remaining sauce, turning to coat.

2. In a 15×10-inch baking pan combine sweet peppers and onion. Drizzle with reserved sauce. Top with chicken.

3. Broil 4 to 5 inches from heat 15 to 18 minutes or until chicken is done (165°F) and vegetables are charred, turning chicken once.

4. Serve sliced chicken and vegetables in tortillas with toppings.

FOR 8 SERVINGS In Step 1, reserve ½ cup of the sauce. In Step 2, use two 15×10-inch baking pans.

PER SERVING *671 cal., 35 g fat (9 g sat. fat), 80 mg chol., 1,039 mg sodium, 57 g carb., 10 g fiber, 33 g pro.*

PREP 20 minutes
BROIL 15 minutes

4 servings	ingredients	8 servings
¼ cup	olive oil	½ cup
3 Tbsp.	lime juice	⅓ cup
3 Tbsp.	Worcestershire sauce	⅓ cup
1 Tbsp + 1 tsp.	chili powder	2 Tbsp. + 2 tsp.
4	cloves garlic, minced	8
1 tsp.	sugar	2 tsp.
½ tsp.	salt	1 tsp.
1 lb.	skinless, boneless chicken breast halves	2 lb.
4 cups	red, green, yellow, and/or orange sweet pepper strips	8 cups
1	medium onion, thinly sliced	2
eight 7- to 8-inch	flour tortillas, warmed	sixteen 7- to 8-inch
	Toppings, such as pico de gallo, chopped avocado, and/or sour cream	

Curried Chicken Salad

For so little effort and time invested, this combination of chicken, crunchy celery, and almonds and the sweetness of raisins in a creamy (but light) curry dressing is a must-have in your recipe repertoire. Serve it in lettuce leaves or tote it for lunch on a split croissant or in a wrap.

1. In a bowl combine chicken, celery, raisins, and almonds. Remove 1 tsp. zest and squeeze 2 Tbsp. juice from orange. For dressing, in a bowl combine mayonnaise, yogurt, orange zest and juice, curry powder, pepper, and salt. Add to chicken mixture; toss gently to coat.

2. Divide lettuce among plates. Top with chicken salad and orange sections.

FOR 8 SERVINGS In Step 1, remove 2 tsp. zest and squeeze 4 Tbsp. juice from orange.

TO MAKE AHEAD Prepare chicken salad as directed in Step 1, except do not add almonds. Cover and chill up to 24 hours. To serve, stir almonds into salad and continue as directed in Step 2.

PER SERVING *419 cal., 14 g fat (2 g sat. fat), 95 mg chol., 434 mg sodium, 36 g carb., 6 g fiber, 39 g pro.*

START TO FINISH 20 minutes

4 servings	ingredients	8 servings
3 cups	shredded cooked chicken breast	6 cups
1½ cups	finely chopped celery	3 cups
½ cup	raisins	1 cup
¼ cup	slivered almonds, toasted (tip, page 19)	½ cup
1	orange	2
½ cup	light mayonnaise	1 cup
⅓ cup	plain fat-free Greek yogurt	⅔ cup
2 tsp.	curry powder or curry paste	4 tsp.
¼ tsp.	cracked black pepper	½ tsp.
⅛ tsp.	salt	¼ tsp.
12	leaf lettuce leaves	24
3	oranges, peeled, sectioned, and seeded	6

Italian Roasted Chicken and Vegetable Toss

Colorful and packed with nutrients, this hybrid between a salad and a hot meal features warm roasted chicken and veggies served on a bed of cool greens.

PREP 25 minutes
ROAST 50 minutes at 375°F

6 servings	ingredients	12 servings
	Nonstick cooking spray	
2 lb.	bone-in chicken breast halves	4 lb.
1 cup	baby carrots	2 cups
8	wedges onion	16
3 cups	1-inch chunks zucchini	6 cups
1 cup	1-inch chunks red or green sweet pepper	2 cups
one 8-oz. pkg.	fresh mushrooms	two 8-oz. pkg.
3 Tbsp.	olive oil	6 Tbsp.
¼ tsp.	salt	½ tsp.
¼ tsp.	black pepper	½ tsp.
2 Tbsp.	balsamic vinegar	¼ cup
1 tsp.	dried Italian seasoning, crushed	2 tsp.
one 8-oz. pkg.	Mediterranean-blend salad greens	two 16-oz. pkg.
¼ cup	Parmesan cheese shards	½ cup

1. Preheat oven to 375°F. Coat a 15×10-inch baking pan with cooking spray. Arrange chicken, skin sides up, in one half of the roasting pan. In the other half arrange carrots and onion wedges. Roast, uncovered, 25 minutes.

2. Remove pan from oven. Add zucchini, sweet pepper, and mushrooms. Drizzle chicken and vegetables with 2 Tbsp. of the oil and sprinkle with the salt and black pepper.

3. Roast, uncovered, 25 minutes or until a thermometer registers 170°F and vegetables are tender. Set chicken aside until cool enough to handle. Transfer vegetables to a bowl.

4. Remove and discard chicken skin and bones. Shred chicken using two forks. Add chicken and any juices in pan to vegetables; toss. In a bowl whisk together vinegar, the remaining olive oil, and Italian seasoning. Add to chicken and vegetables; toss to coat.

5. Arrange greens on serving platter; top with chicken and vegetables. Sprinkle with cheese.

FOR 12 SERVINGS Use two 15×10-inch baking pans. In Step 2, use 4 Tbsp. of the oil.

PER SERVING *219 cal., 10 g fat (2 g sat. fat), 51 mg chol., 217 mg sodium, 10 g carb., 2 g fiber, 22 g pro.*

Mexican Corn-Chicken Casserole

Cooking the rice in chicken broth gives it a flavor boost. You can use the same trick when you are cooking rice as a simple side dish. Stir in fresh herbs or sliced green onions for added interest.

1. Preheat oven to 350°F. Grease an 8×8-inch baking dish. In a large saucepan combine broth and rice. Bring to boiling; reduce heat. Simmer, covered, 15 minutes or until rice is tender.

2. Meanwhile, in another large saucepan heat oil over medium heat. Add chopped onion and garlic; cook until onion is tender, stirring occasionally. Remove from heat.

3. Stir in corn, tomatoes, chicken, tomato sauce, half the cheese, the chili powder, and cooked rice. Transfer to prepared dish. Sprinkle with the remaining cheese.

4. Bake 20 to 25 minutes or until heated through and cheese is lightly browned. If desired, top with sour cream, green onions, and/or cilantro.

FOR 8 SERVINGS Use a 9×13-inch baking dish.

PER SERVING *524 cal., 16 g fat (7 g sat. fat), 70 mg chol., 1,099 mg sodium, 66 g carb., 6 g fiber, 32 g pro.*

PREP 35 minutes
BAKE 20 minutes at 350°F

4 servings	ingredients	8 servings
one 14.5-oz. can	reduced-sodium chicken broth	two 14.5-oz. cans
1 cup	uncooked long grain rice	2 cups
1 Tbsp.	vegetable oil	2 Tbsp.
¼ cup	chopped onion	½ cup
2	cloves garlic, minced	4
2 cups	frozen corn, thawed	4 cups
one 14.5-oz. can	diced tomatoes, undrained	two 14.5-oz. cans
1½ cups	shredded cooked chicken breast	3 cups
1 cup	tomato sauce	2 cups
1 cup	shredded Mexican four-cheese blend	2 cups
1 Tbsp.	chili powder	2 Tbsp.
	Sour cream, thinly sliced green onions, and/or fresh cilantro sprigs (optional)	

Peanut Chicken Satay Stir-Fry

This quick dish takes its inspiration from the Indonesian specialty of chicken or meat grilled on a stick and served with a sweet, peanutty, and spicy dipping sauce. The addition of vegetables and rice makes it a meal.

1. For sauce, in a bowl whisk together coconut milk, peanut butter, the ½ tsp. salt, ginger, and crushed red pepper.

2. Lightly season chicken with additional salt and black pepper. In a large skillet or wok heat oil over medium-high heat. Add chicken; cook 6 minutes or until no longer pink, turning once. Remove from skillet.

3. Add stir-fry vegetables and peas to hot skillet. Cook and stir 2 to 3 minutes or until heated through.

4. Add sauce to skillet; return chicken to skillet. Stir together and heat through. Serve stir-fry over hot cooked rice.

FOR 8 SERVINGS In Step 1, use 1 tsp. salt.

PER SERVING *754 cal., 37 g fat (15 g sat. fat), 73 mg chol., 836 mg sodium, 64 g carb., 5 g fiber, 42 g pro.*

START TO FINISH 25 minutes

4 servings	ingredients	8 servings
one 14-oz. can	unsweetened light coconut milk	two 14-oz. cans
⅓ cup	peanut butter	⅔ cup
½ tsp.	salt	1 tsp.
½ tsp.	ground ginger	1 tsp.
¼ tsp.	crushed red pepper	½ tsp.
1 lb.	skinless, boneless chicken breast halves, cut into 1-inch pieces	2 lb.
	Salt and black pepper	
1 Tbsp.	canola oil or vegetable oil	2 Tbsp.
2 cups	frozen stir-fry vegetables	4 cups
½ cup	frozen peas	1 cup
4 cups	hot cooked brown or white rice	8 cups

Warm Brussels Sprouts Salad with Chicken

The combination of the warm, cabbagey sprouts and cool, sweet oranges provides balance to this fresh and healthful salad. It's perfect for a late fall supper; both Brussels sprouts and oranges are at peak season at that time of year.

1. Sprinkle chicken with salt and pepper. Grill chicken, covered, over medium heat for 12 to 15 minutes or until chicken is done (165°F), turning once.

2. Meanwhile, in a large skillet heat half the oil over medium heat. Add Brussels sprouts, onion, and celery. Cook, covered, 4 to 6 minutes or until sprouts are crisp-tender, stirring occasionally. Cook, uncovered, 2 to 3 minutes more or until sprouts are lightly browned, stirring occasionally.

3. In a small bowl whisk together remaining oil, vinegar, mustard, and sage; pour over sprouts mixture. Cook and stir 1 minute more.

4. Thinly slice chicken. Serve warm salad with chicken, oranges, walnuts, and additional sage.

PER SERVING *399 cal., 22 g fat (3 g sat. fat), 103 mg chol., 471 mg sodium, 14 g carb., 5 g fiber, 36 g pro.*

START TO FINISH 40 minutes

4 servings	ingredients	8 servings
1¼ lb.	skinless, boneless chicken breast halves	2½ lb.
½ tsp.	sea salt	1 tsp.
¼ tsp.	freshly ground black pepper	½ tsp.
¼ cup	olive oil	½ cup
one 9-oz. pkg.	shaved Brussels sprouts	two 9-oz. pkg.
½ cup	thinly sliced red onion	1 cup
½ cup	thinly sliced celery	1 cup
¼ cup	cider vinegar	½ cup
1 Tbsp.	Dijon mustard	2 Tbsp.
2 tsp.	snipped fresh sage	4 tsp.
2	small oranges, peeled and thinly sliced	4
¼ cup	chopped toasted walnuts, toasted (tip, page 19)	½ cup

Greek Chicken and Pita Casserole

Seasoned pita wedges make a crispy "crust" for this quick casserole. A topping of tomatoes, cheese, and olives goes on after it comes out of the oven.

6 servings	ingredients	12 servings
4 cups	chopped cooked chicken or turkey	8 cups
3	medium zucchini, halved lengthwise and cut into ½-inch pieces (4 cups)	6
one 10.75-oz. can	condensed cream of chicken soup	two 10.75-oz. cans
½ cup	chopped red onion	1 cup
½ cup	chicken broth	1 cup
1½ tsp.	Greek seasoning	3 tsp.
2	cloves garlic, minced	4
two 6-inch	pita bread rounds, cut into small wedges	four 6-inch
	Nonstick cooking spray	
1 cup	chopped roma tomatoes	2 cups
1 cup	crumbled feta cheese	2 cups
½ cup	pitted Kalamata olives, sliced	1 cup

1. Preheat oven to 400°F. In a bowl combine the first five ingredients (through broth), 1 tsp. of the Greek seasoning, and the garlic. Transfer to a 9×13-inch baking dish.

2. Coat pita wedges with cooking spray; sprinkle with the remaining Greek seasoning. Top with pita wedges. Bake, uncovered, 25 minutes or until heated through. Top with tomatoes, cheese, and olives.

FOR 12 SERVINGS Use two 9×13-inch baking dishes. In Step 1, use 2 tsp. of the Greek seasoning.

PER SERVING *407 cal., 19 g fat (7 g sat. fat), 109 mg chol., 1,185 mg sodium, 22 g carb., 2 g fiber, 35 g pro.*

Greek Chicken Kabobs

Got less than 30 minutes to get dinner on the table? Tuck into these lemony herbed chicken kabobs served in pita flatbreads.

PREP 15 minutes
BROIL 12 minutes

4 servings	ingredients	8 servings
	Nonstick cooking spray	
1	lemon	2
3 Tbsp.	snipped fresh oregano	⅓ cup
2 Tbsp.	olive oil	¼ cup
2	cloves garlic, minced	4
¾ tsp.	salt	1½ tsp.
¼ tsp.	black pepper	½ tsp.
1½ lb.	chicken breast tenderloins	3 lb.
1 cup	grape tomatoes	2 cups
one 6-oz. carton	plain low-fat yogurt	two 6-oz. cartons
½ cup	shredded cucumber	1 cup
4	Greek pita flatbreads	8

1. Preheat broiler. Line a 15×10-inch baking pan with foil. Lightly coat foil with cooking spray.

2. Remove 2 tsp. zest and squeeze 4 Tbsp. juice from lemon. Reserve 1 Tbsp. of the lemon juice. In a bowl whisk together lemon zest, 3 Tbsp. juice, oregano, oil, garlic, ½ tsp. of the salt, and the pepper. Add chicken; toss to coat. Thread chicken and tomatoes onto six to eight long metal skewers. Place kabobs in prepared baking pan; drizzle with remaining lemon mixture.

3. Broil 4 to 5 inches from the heat for 12 to 14 minutes or until chicken is done (165°F), turning once.

4. Meanwhile, in a bowl combine yogurt, cucumber, the reserved lemon juice, and the remaining salt.

5. Remove chicken and tomatoes from skewers. Spread yogurt mixture on flatbreads. Top with chicken and tomatoes.

FOR 8 SERVINGS If necessary, use two 15×10-inch baking pans. In Step 2, remove 4 tsp. zest and squeeze ½ cup juice from lemons, reserving 2 Tbsp. juice.

PER SERVING *514 cal., 14 g fat (2 g sat. fat), 111 mg chol., 1,068 mg sodium, 49 g carb., 7 g fiber, 47 g pro.*

Chicken Alfredo Cauliflower Rice Bake

Having a hard time getting kids to eat their veggies? They will gobble them down in this homey dish featuring chicken, spinach, cheese, and cauliflower "rice" baked in a light Alfredo sauce and topped with crispy bread crumbs. Yum!

1. Preheat oven to 400°F. Working in batches, cover and pulse cauliflower in a food processor until crumbly and resembles rice.

2. Transfer cauliflower to a 9×13-inch baking dish or casserole. Drizzle with half the oil and sprinkle with basil, salt, and pepper; toss to coat. Bake, uncovered, 15 minutes.

3. Stir in spinach, chicken, and pasta sauce; sprinkle with cheese. Stir together panko and the remaining oil; sprinkle over casserole. Bake 20 to 25 minutes more or until top is browned.

FOR 12 SERVINGS Use two 9×13-inch dishes.

PER SERVING *255 cal., 16 g fat (6 g sat. fat), 83 mg chol., 743 mg sodium, 12 g carb., 2 g fiber, 17 g pro.*

PREP 20 minutes
BAKE 35 minutes at 400°F

6 servings	ingredients	12 servings
one 2¼- to 2½-lb.	head cauliflower, trimmed and broken into florets	two 2¼- to 2½-lb.
¼ cup	olive oil	½ cup
1 tsp.	dried basil, crushed	2 tsp.
¼ tsp.	salt	½ tsp.
¼ tsp.	black pepper	½ tsp.
2½ cups	fresh baby spinach	5 cups
2 cups	chopped rotisserie chicken	4 cups
one 14.5-oz. jar	light Alfredo pasta sauce	two 14.5-oz. jars
2 Tbsp.	grated Parmesan cheese	¼ cup
½ cup	panko bread crumbs	1 cup

Coconut-Curry Noodle Bowl

Use a regular curry powder for a mild flavor—or Madras-style or hot curry powder (or half and half) if you like a little heat.

1. In a large saucepan heat oil over medium heat. Add carrots and garlic; cook 4 to 5 minutes or until carrots are crisp-tender, stirring occasionally.

2. Stir in the next seven ingredients (through pepper). Bring to boiling; reduce heat. Simmer, covered, 3 minutes. Stir in chicken; heat through. If desired, sprinkle with peanuts.

PER SERVING *475 cal., 35 g fat (23 g sat. fat), 52 mg chol., 677 mg sodium, 22 g carb., 2 g fiber, 20 g pro.*

START TO FINISH 25 minutes

4 servings	ingredients	8 servings
1 Tbsp.	vegetable oil	2 Tbsp.
1 cup	thinly sliced carrots	2 cups
3	cloves garlic, minced	6
one 14.5-oz. can	chicken broth	two 14.5-oz. cans
one 14-oz. can	unsweetened coconut milk	two 14-oz. cans
1 cup	broccoli florets	2 cups
one 3-oz. pkg.	ramen noodles, coarsely broken (discard seasoning packet)	two 3-oz. pkg.
2 tsp.	curry powder	4 tsp.
¼ tsp.	salt	½ tsp.
¼ tsp.	black pepper	½ tsp.
1½ cups	shredded cooked chicken	3 cups
	Chopped peanuts (optional)	

Honey-Sriracha Grilled Chicken Thighs

Spicy and sweet, these juicy chicken thighs are perfect paired with blistered green beans or a crisp Asian-style slaw. Toss together packaged broccoli slaw with a bottled sesame-ginger vinaigrette and dinner is done!

1. Whisk together 2 Tbsp. of the sriracha sauce and the honey; set aside. Place chicken in a resealable plastic bag and add remaining sriracha sauce and lime juice. Seal; turn bag to coat chicken. Let stand 15 minutes.

2. Grill chicken on a greased rack, covered, over medium heat for 30 to 35 minutes or until done (175°F), turning three or four times.

3. Place chicken on a platter; brush with sriracha-honey sauce. Cover and let stand 5 minutes. Sprinkle with cilantro.

FOR 8 SERVINGS In Step 1, use 4 Tbsp. sriracha sauce.

PER SERVING *300 cal., 8 g fat (2 g sat. fat), 191 mg chol., 426 mg sodium, 14 g carb., 0 g fiber, 40 g pro.*

PREP 15 minutes
STAND 20 minutes
GRILL 30 minutes

4 servings	ingredients	8 servings
6 Tbsp.	sriracha sauce	¾ cup
2 Tbsp.	honey	¼ cup
8	bone-in chicken thighs, skinned	16
2 Tbsp.	fresh lime juice	¼ cup
2 Tbsp.	chopped fresh cilantro	¼ cup

Nacho Chicken Drummettes

These tortilla-and-cheese-coated drummies can be served as either a main course or as an appetizer.

1. Preheat oven to 400°F. Line a 15×10-inch baking pan with foil. Grease foil; set pan aside. Pour the taco sauce into a shallow dish. Place tortilla chips in another shallow dish. Dip chicken into taco sauce, then into tortilla chips, turning to coat. Place chicken in the prepared pan.

2. Bake 30 to 40 minutes or until chicken is done (175°F). Do not turn chicken while baking. If desired, sprinkle with cheese and serve with dipping sauce(s).

FOR 12 SERVINGS Use two 15×10-inch baking pans.

*TIP Alternatively, for 6 servings, substitute 12 drumsticks. For 12 servings, substitute 24 drumsticks.

PER SERVING *603 cal., 40 g fat (10 g sat. fat), 112 mg chol., 609 mg sodium, 29 g carb., 2 g fiber, 31 g pro.*

PREP 15 minutes
BAKE 30 minutes at 400°F

6 servings	ingredients	12 servings
1½ cups	mild taco sauce	3 cups
4 cups	crushed tortilla chips	8 cups
3 lb.	chicken drummettes*	6 lb.
	Shredded Mexican cheese blend (optional)	
	Dipping sauce(s) such as ranch salad dressing, salsa, taco sauce, and/or barbecue sauce (optional)	

Butter Beans, Italian Sausage, and Chard

Butter beans earned their name for their rich, creamy texture and taste. If you can't find them, you can substitute cannellini beans.

1. In an extra-large skillet heat oil over medium heat. Add sausage and onion wedges; cook and stir 6 to 8 minutes or until browned.

2. Add oregano and garlic to skillet; cook 1 minute. Add broth. Bring to boiling; reduce heat. Boil gently, uncovered, 3 to 4 minutes or until reduced by about half. Gradually add greens, tossing until wilted before adding more. Add butter beans and vinegar; heat through. Sprinkle with cheese.

PER SERVING *314 cal., 12 g fat (4 g sat. fat), 69 mg chol., 1,311 mg sodium, 24 g carb, 6 g fiber, 26 g pro.*

START TO FINISH 30 minutes

4 servings	ingredients	8 servings
1 Tbsp.	olive oil	2 Tbsp.
four 3-oz.	cooked sweet Italian chicken sausage links, cut up	eight 3-oz.
1	medium onion, cut into thin wedges	2
2 Tbsp.	fresh oregano leaves	¼ cup
2	cloves garlic, minced	4
1 cup	reduced-sodium chicken broth	2 cups
12 cups	fresh Swiss chard, stemmed and torn	24 cups
one 15- to 16-oz. can	butter beans, rinsed and drained	two 15- to 16-oz. cans
2 Tbsp.	balsamic vinegar	¼ cup
	Shaved Parmesan cheese	

Chicken and Spinach Phyllo Bake

Spanakopita, the classic Greek pastry-encased casserole, gets a protein boost in this recipe with the addition of ground chicken.

1. Preheat oven to 375°F. Lightly coat a 9×13-inch baking dish with cooking spray.

2. In an extra-large skillet melt butter over medium-high heat. Add ground chicken and onion; cook 8 minutes or until chicken is browned and onion is tender. Drain off fat. Stir in the next five ingredients (through crushed red pepper); cook and stir 5 minutes. Transfer to a large bowl. Stir in eggs, cheese, and oregano.

3. Unfold phyllo dough. Using a sharp knife, cut a 1-inch strip from one short end of the phyllo stack; discard. Place a phyllo sheet in the bottom of the prepared dish; lightly coat phyllo with cooking spray. Top with seven more sheets, coating each sheet with cooking spray. Spread chicken mixture over phyllo in dish. Top with the remaining phyllo sheets, coating each sheet with cooking spray and casually crumpling the top few sheets.

4. Bake, uncovered, 45 minutes or until heated through and phyllo is golden.

FOR 16 SERVINGS Use two 9×13-inch baking pans.

PER SERVING *530 cal., 29 g fat (13 g sat. fat), 273 mg chol., 1,024 mg sodium, 29 g carb., 4 g fiber, 41 g pro.*

PREP 35 minutes
BAKE 45 minutes at 375°F

8 servings	ingredients	16 servings
	Nonstick cooking spray	
2 Tbsp.	butter	¼ cup
2½ lb.	uncooked ground chicken	5 lb.
1 cup	chopped onion	2 cups
three 10-oz. pkg.	frozen chopped spinach, thawed and squeezed dry	six 10-oz. pkg.
1 tsp.	black pepper	2 tsp.
½ tsp.	salt	1 tsp.
½ tsp.	ground nutmeg	1 tsp.
¼ tsp.	crushed red pepper	½ tsp.
4	eggs, lightly beaten	8
6 oz.	crumbled feta cheese	12 oz.
1 Tbsp.	snipped fresh oregano	2 Tbsp.
16 sheets	frozen phyllo dough (14×9-inch rectangles), thawed	32 sheets

Rosemary and Ravioli Chicken Soup

A tiny bit of butter stirred into this light, spring-inspired soup right before serving gives it wonderful flavor and aroma.

4 servings	ingredients	8 servings
one 32-oz. carton	reduced-sodium vegetable broth	two 32-oz. cartons
1 cup	water	2 cups
1½ cups	coarsely chopped red-skin potatoes	3 cups
1 Tbsp.	snipped fresh rosemary	2 Tbsp.
one 9- to 12-oz. pkg.	refrigerated spinach or mushroom ravioli	two 9- to 12-oz. pkg.
½	rotisserie chicken, meat removed and cut up	1
8 oz.	fresh green beans, trimmed and cut into 2-inch pieces	1 lb.
1 Tbsp.	butter	2 Tbsp.
	Cracked black pepper	

1. In a 4- to 6-qt. Dutch oven bring vegetable broth and water to boiling over medium-high heat. Add potatoes and rosemary; return to boiling. Reduce heat and cook, covered, 10 minutes.

2. Add ravioli, chicken, and green beans to pot with potatoes. Return to boiling; reduce heat. Simmer, covered, 5 to 7 minutes or until pasta and potatoes are tender. Stir in butter. Top servings with additional snipped fresh rosemary and cracked black pepper.

FOR 8 SERVINGS Use a 6- to 8-qt. Dutch oven.

PER SERVING *381 cal., 13 g fat (5 g sat. fat), 124 mg chol., 1,098 mg sodium, 38 g carb., 4 g fiber, 28 g pro.*

Chicken Tortilla Soup

Jarred black bean and corn salsa and frozen fire-roasted sweet peppers make the trip to soup satisfaction a quick one in this take on the traditional Mexican favorite.

1. In a 4-qt. Dutch oven combine first six ingredients (through oregano). Bring to boiling; reduce heat. Simmer 5 minutes or until heated through, stirring occasionally.

2. Top servings with tortilla chips and, if desired, sour cream.

FOR 12 SERVINGS Use a 6- to 8-qt. Dutch oven.

*TIP In place of frozen fire-roasted peppers, you can substitute one 14.4-oz. pkg. frozen pepper stir-fry vegetables (green, red, and yellow sweet peppers and onion).

PER SERVING *217 cal., 7 g fat (1 g sat. fat), 53 mg chol., 737 mg sodium, 25 g carb., 6 g fiber, 17 g pro.*

START TO FINISH 25 minutes

6 servings	ingredients	12 servings
2 cups	shredded rotisserie chicken	4 cups
2 cups	water	4 cups
one 15.5- to 16-oz. jar	black bean and corn salsa	two 15.5- to 16-oz. jars
one 14.5-oz. can	reduced-sodium chicken broth	two 14.5-oz. cans
one 12-oz. pkg.	frozen fire-roasted tricolor peppers, such as Green Giant	two 12-oz. pkg.
2 tsp.	dried oregano, crushed	4 tsp.
	Coarsely crushed tortilla chips	
	Sour cream (optional)	

Sweet-Spicy Barbecue Chicken Sliders

These sweet and spicy sliders can be made up to 8 hours ahead. When it's party time, just drizzle with butter and bake until melty.

1. Preheat oven to 350°F. Arrange roll bottoms in an 8×8-inch baking pan. In a bowl combine the next four ingredients (through pickled jalapeño peppers). Spoon onto roll bottoms. Top with cheese and roll tops.

2. In a bowl combine butter, honey, Worcestershire sauce, and black pepper. Drizzle over rolls.

3. Bake, covered, 15 minutes. Uncover; bake 10 to 15 minutes more or until cheese is melted and roll tops are light brown.

FOR 12 SERVINGS Use a 9×13-inch baking pan.

TO MAKE AHEAD Assemble sandwiches and do not drizzle with butter mixture. Cover and refrigerate up to 8 hours. Drizzle and bake as directed.

PER SERVING *390 cal., 15 g fat (7 g sat. fat), 71 mg chol., 603 mg sodium, 40 g carb., 1 g fiber, 23 g pro.*

PREP 20 minutes
BAKE 25 minutes at 350°F

6 servings	ingredients	12 servings
six 3-inch	sandwich rolls	twelve 3-inch
1¼ cups	shredded cooked chicken breast	2½ cups
½ cup	chopped fresh or canned pineapple, well drained	1 cup
⅓ cup	barbecue sauce	⅔ cup
2 Tbsp.	chopped pickled jalapeño peppers	¼ cup
¾ cup	shredded Monterrey Jack cheese	1½ cups
3 Tbsp.	melted butter	6 Tbsp.
1 Tbsp.	honey	2 Tbsp.
1½ tsp.	Worcestershire sauce	1 Tbsp.
¼ tsp.	black pepper	½ tsp.
	Sliced jalapeño peppers (tip, page 12) (optional)	

4 servings	ingredients	8 servings
1 lb.	skinless, boneless chicken breast halves	2 lb.
1 Tbsp.	vegetable oil	2 Tbsp.
3	medium carrots, thinly bias-sliced	6
3	stalks celery, thinly bias-sliced	6
4 oz.	blue cheese, crumbled	8 oz.
½ cup	barbecue sauce	1 cup
½ tsp.	hot pepper sauce	1 tsp.
two 13.8-oz. pkg.	refrigerated pizza dough	four 13.8-oz. pkg.
1	egg, beaten	2

Buffalo Chicken Rolls

For game day or any day, these knife-and-fork rolls are stuffed with all things Buffalo—chicken, carrots, celery, blue cheese, and a bbq-style spicy hot pepper sauce.

1. Preheat oven to 375°F. Line a 15×10-inch baking pan with parchment.

2. For the filling, in large skillet cook chicken in hot oil over medium heat 6 minutes. Turn chicken; add carrots and celery to skillet. Cover and cook 6 to 8 minutes or until chicken is done (165°F) and vegetables are crisp-tender. Cool slightly, then use two forks to shred chicken. In a large bowl combine shredded chicken, cooked carrots and celery, ⅓ cup of the barbecue sauce, and hot pepper sauce.

3. Unroll one package pizza dough and cut into four 4×6-inch rectangles. Divide half of the filling among rectangles, leaving a 1-inch border on each long side. Sprinkle with half of the cheese. Brush edges of dough with some of the egg. Fold one of the long sides of dough over filling; seal seam with tines of a fork. Place rolls in prepared baking pan. Repeat with remaining dough, filling, cheese, and egg.

4. Bake, uncovered, 23 to 25 minutes or until golden brown, brushing with barbecue sauce the last 5 minutes. Serve with additional cheese, barbecue sauce, and celery.

FOR 8 SERVINGS In Step 2, use ⅔ cup of the barbecue sauce.

PER SERVING *814 cal., 20 g fat (9 g sat. fat), 87 mg chol., 2,104 mg sodium, 110 g carb., 5 g fiber, 49 g pro.*

Ham, Cheese, and Turkey Stromboli

Stromboli is essentially a spiral-rolled pizza that lends itself to all kinds of stuffing combinations— start with this version and then get creative with some of your favorites.

1. Preheat oven to 375°F. Lightly brush a baking sheet with oil; sprinkle with cornmeal.

2. On a lightly floured surface roll pizza dough into a 13×10-inch rectangle. Arrange ham slices on dough to within ½ inch of edges. Sprinkle with half the cheese. Layer spinach and turkey on cheese. Top with the remaining cheese, the sweet pepper, and olives. Starting from a long side, roll up dough; pinch to seal seams.

3. Place loaf, seam side down, on prepared baking sheet. Brush with egg; cut a few slits in top for steam to escape. Bake 30 minutes or until golden. Cool slightly. If desired, serve with marinara sauce.

FOR 8 SERVINGS Use two baking sheets and roll each pizza dough around filling.

PER SERVING *417 cal., 17 g fat (5 g sat. fat), 93 mg chol., 1,290 mg sodium, 44 g carb., 3 g fiber, 23 g pro.*

PREP 20 minutes
BAKE 30 minutes at 375°F

4 servings	ingredients	8 servings
1 tsp.	olive oil	2 tsp.
1 Tbsp.	cornmeal	2 Tbsp.
one 13.8-oz. pkg.	refrigerated pizza dough	two 13.8-oz. pkg.
4 oz.	thinly sliced cooked ham	8 oz.
1 cup	shredded mozzarella cheese	2 cups
1 cup	fresh baby spinach or torn spinach leaves	2 cups
4 oz.	thinly sliced cooked turkey	8 oz.
⅓ cup	chopped red, green, or yellow sweet pepper	⅔ cup
¼ cup	Kalamata olives, pitted and chopped	½ cup
1	egg, lightly beaten	2
	Warm marinara sauce or pizza sauce (optional)	

Overgrown Garden Turkey Melt

Get your hands (and your mouth) around this generously stuffed veggie melt bursting with lean smoked turkey, artichoke hearts, tomato, and spinach and slathered with a garlic-rosemary mayo.

1. Preheat oven to 400°F. In a bowl combine mayonnaise, rosemary, and garlic. Stir in spinach and artichokes.

2. Remove bread from each half to create a 1-inch shell. Lay each half on a baking sheet. Line with cheese, tearing to cover as necessary. Spoon the spinach mixture on cheese. Top with tomato and turkey.

3. Bake 10 minutes or until toasted and heated through. Put halves together, cut each in half, and, if desired, secure with wooden pick.

PER SERVING *495 cal., 19 g fat (7 g sat. fat), 40 mg chol., 1,275 mg sodium, 55 g carb., 4 g fiber, 28 g pro.*

PREP 20 minutes
BAKE 10 minutes at 400°F

4 servings	ingredients	8 servings
3 Tbsp.	mayonnaise	⅓ cup
2 tsp.	chopped fresh rosemary	4 tsp.
2	cloves garlic, minced	4
2 cups	fresh spinach, coarsely chopped	4 cups
one 14-oz. can	artichoke hearts, drained, chopped, and patted dry	two 14-oz. cans
two 8-oz. loaves	Ciabatta, French, or Italian bread (not baguettes), halved lengthwise	four 8-oz. loaves
8 slices	mozzarella cheese	16 slices
1	medium tomato, thinly sliced	2
4 oz.	sliced smoked turkey	8 oz.

Tarragon-Blue Cheese Turkey Patties

Tarragon, with a mild licorice taste, is a natural with poultry. If you can't find it—or if you're not a fan—you can substitute fresh basil.

1. In a small bowl stir together the honey and mustard. In a large bowl combine the turkey, half the blue cheese, the chopped red onion, chopped tarragon, and hot pepper sauce. Shape into four ¾-inch-thick patties.

2. Grill patties on a greased rack, covered, over medium heat for 12 to 15 minutes or until done (165°F), turning once. Serve on buns with remaining blue cheese, lettuce, and onion slices. Top with honey-mustard and additional tarragon.

PER SERVING *390 cal., 19 g fat (7 g sat. fat), 99 mg chol., 944 mg sodium, 26 g carb., 4 g fiber, 25 g pro.*

PREP 20 minutes
GRILL 12 minutes

4 servings	ingredients	8 servings
2 tsp.	honey	4 tsp.
2 Tbsp.	Dijon coarse ground mustard	¼ cup
1 lb.	ground turkey	2 lb.
2 oz.	blue cheese, crumbled	4 oz.
¼ cup	finely chopped red onion	½ cup
1 tsp.	chopped fresh tarragon	2 tsp.
1 to 2 tsp.	bottled hot pepper sauce	2 to 4 tsp.
4	sandwich buns, split and toasted	8
4	leaves lettuce	8
	Thinly sliced red onion	

CHAPTER 3

Meat

Whether you're in the mood for steak, stew, sausage, or a sandwich, these entrées featuring beef or pork are hearty and satisfying.

70 Espresso-Marinated Flank Steak

72 Steak with Spicy Balsamic Glaze

73 Beef Stew Pot Pie

74 Brunswick Stew

75 Orange Teriyaki Beef Stew

77 Italian Roast Beef Slider Melts

78 Tacos in Pasta Shells

81 Mini Meat Loaves with Potatoes and Beans

82 Pork Chops with Roasted Vegetables and Balsamic Drizzle

84 Ginger-Soy Pork Chops on Greens

85 Spicy Skillet Pork Chops

86 Pork Cassoulet

87 Pork and Potatoes with Minted Yogurt

89 Pork and Squash Enchiladas

90 Spicy Asian Pork Cabbage Rolls

93 Roasted Sausage with Mushrooms, Squash, and Polenta

95 Sweet Potato-Chorizo Lasagna

96 Zoodle Pizza Casserole

97 Creamy Alfredo with Bacon and Peas

99 Egg Baguette Bake

100 Roasted Pear-Ham Melts

102 Smoky Pizza Melts

103 Cajun Sausage-Potato Soup

105 Pork and Wild Rice Soup

77

97

99

Espresso-Marinated Flank Steak

This tasty steak has a double shot of espresso to give it wide-awake flavor. It features chilled coffee in the marinade and instant espresso powder rubbed over the surface before grilling.

PREP 20 minutes
MARINATE 4 hours
GRILL 17 minutes

4 servings	ingredients	8 servings
one 1½- to 2-lb.	beef flank steak	two 1½- to 2-lb.
1 cup	espresso coffee, chilled	2 cups
¼ cup	finely chopped red onion	½ cup
2 Tbsp.	packed brown sugar	¼ cup
2 Tbsp.	Dijon mustard	¼ cup
2 Tbsp.	balsamic vinegar	¼ cup
1 Tbsp.	olive oil	2 Tbsp.
1 tsp.	cracked black pepper	2 tsp.
2	cloves garlic, minced	4
1 tsp.	instant espresso coffee powder	2 tsp.
¼ tsp.	salt	½ tsp.
¼ tsp.	black pepper	½ tsp.
	Grilled French bread (optional)	

1. Trim fat from steak. Score both sides of steak in a diamond pattern by making shallow diagonal cuts at 1-inch intervals. Place steak in a large resealable plastic bag set in a shallow dish.

2. For marinade, in a small bowl combine the next eight ingredients (through garlic). Pour marinade over steak in bag; seal bag. Turn to coat steak. Marinate in the refrigerator 4 to 12 hours, turning bag occasionally.

3. Drain steak, discarding marinade. Sprinkle espresso powder over both sides of steak; rub in with your fingers.

4. Grill steak, uncovered, over medium heat 17 to 21 minutes for medium (160°F), turning once.

5. Sprinkle steak with salt and pepper. Thinly slice steak diagonally across the grain. Serve with grilled French bread if desired.

PER SERVING *271 cal., 12 g fat (5 g sat. fat), 60 mg chol., 253 mg sodium, 1 g carb., 0 g fiber, 36 g pro.*

Steak with Spicy Balsamic Glaze

Serve this spicy-sweet steak with a simple salad of baby spinach and sliced fresh peaches or nectarines drizzled with your favorite vinaigrette.

PREP 25 minutes
STAND 20 minutes
COOK 19 minutes

4 servings	ingredients	8 servings
1 lb.	boneless beef top sirloin steak, about 1 inch thick, trimmed of fat	2 lb.
½ cup	water	1 cup
½ cup	apple cider	1 cup
¼ cup	Worcestershire sauce	½ cup
¼ cup	balsamic vinegar	½ cup
¼ tsp.	crushed red pepper	½ tsp.
	Nonstick cooking spray	
	Salt and black pepper	
¼ cup	honey	½ cup

1. Place steak in a resealable plastic bag. Add water, apple cider, Worcestershire, balsamic vinegar, and crushed red pepper. Seal bag, turning to coat meat. Let stand 20 minutes, turning occasionally.

2. Coat a large skillet with cooking spray; heat over medium heat. Remove beef from marinade, reserving marinade. Season beef with salt and black pepper. Cook in skillet 12 minutes, turning once, or until desired doneness. Remove to a cutting board; cover.

3. Add marinade and honey to skillet; whisk to combine. Bring to boiling; boil gently, uncovered, 7 minutes or until reduced to ⅓ cup. Serve glaze with sliced steak.

FOR 8 SERVINGS In Step 3, reduce glaze to ⅔ cup.

PER SERVING *286 cal., 5 g fat (2 g sat. fat), 68 mg chol., 384 mg sodium, 34 g carb., 1 g fiber, 26 g pro.*

Beef Stew Pot Pie

This warming dish is perfect for a cold weeknight when you want some serious comfort food but don't have much time to get dinner on the table.

1. Preheat oven to 375°F. Coat an 8×8-inch baking dish with cooking spray.

2. In a small bowl microwave 1½ tsp. of the butter on medium-high 30 seconds or until melted. Brush cut sides of croissants with melted butter. Cube croissants.

3. In a large skillet melt the remaining butter over medium heat. Add carrots, celery, and onions. Cook 7 to 9 minutes or just until vegetables are tender, stirring occasionally. Carefully stir in the next seven ingredients (through pepper). Bring to boiling; reduce heat. Simmer, uncovered, 5 minutes. Stir in beef with gravy and the broth; heat through.

4. Transfer hot stew to the prepared dish. Sprinkle with cubed croissants. Bake, uncovered, 20 to 25 minutes or until bubbly and croissants are golden.

FOR 8 SERVINGS Use a 9×13-inch baking dish. In Step 2, use 1 Tbsp. of the butter.

PER SERVING *330 cal., 16 g fat (8 g sat. fat), 77 mg chol., 885 mg sodium, 21 g carb., 3 g fiber, 21 g pro.*

PREP 25 minutes
BAKE 20 minutes at 375°F

4 servings	ingredients	8 servings
	Nonstick cooking spray	
2 Tbsp.	butter	¼ cup
1½	croissants, split	3
¾ cup	coarsely chopped carrots	1½ cups
¾ cup	coarsely chopped celery	1½ cups
½ cup	frozen small whole onions, thawed and halved	1 cup
1½ cups	sliced fresh mushrooms	3 cups
½ cup	Burgundy or dry red wine	1 cup
1½ tsp.	stone-ground Dijon mustard	1 Tbsp.
2	cloves garlic, minced	4
1 tsp.	finely snipped fresh rosemary	2 tsp.
2 tsp.	dried thyme, crushed	4 tsp.
½ tsp.	black pepper	1 tsp.
two 17-oz. pkg.	refrigerated cooked beef tips with gravy	four 17-oz. pkg.
1 cup	50%-less-sodium beef broth	2 cups

Brunswick Stew

The base of this super-quick-to-fix stew is a package of refrigerated cooked roast beef and a package of refrigerated cooked shredded pork. The result: deliciously hearty food made in a heartbeat.

1. In a 4-qt. Dutch oven combine first seven ingredients (through Worcestershire sauce). Bring just to boiling; reduce heat. Simmer 15 to 20 minutes or until potatoes are tender, stirring occasionally. If desired, serve with mini corn bread muffins.

FOR 12 SERVINGS Use a 6- to 8-qt. Dutch oven.

PER SERVING *269 cal., 6 g fat (3 g sat. fat), 46 mg chol., 922 mg sodium, 38 g carb., 4 g fiber, 21 g pro.*

PREP 15 minutes
COOK 15 minutes

6 servings	ingredients	12 servings
4 cups	water	8 cups
one 28-oz. can	fire-roasted crushed tomatoes	two 28-oz. cans
2 cups	frozen diced hash brown potatoes with onions and peppers	4 cups
2 cups	frozen whole kernel corn and/or lima beans	4 cups
one 15-oz. pkg.	refrigerated cooked beef roast au jus, broken into chunks	two 15-oz. pkg.
half 16-oz. pkg.	refrigerated cooked shredded pork with bbq sauce	one 16-oz. pkg.
1 Tbsp.	Worcestershire sauce	2 Tbsp.
	Mini corn bread muffins or corn bread sticks (optional)	

Orange Teriyaki Beef Stew

This aromatic one-pot meal takes the flavors of a favorite stir-fry and translates them to a saucy stew that simmers for up to an hour while you do other things. Adding the bok choy leaves the last 5 minutes of cooking keeps them fresh and bright green.

1. Toss beef with five-spice powder and salt. Heat oil in a 4-qt. Dutch oven over medium-high heat. Add beef in batches and sear until browned all over, 5 to 8 minutes. Remove to a plate.

2. Add mushrooms and white bok choy stems (reserve green leaves) and cook 2 minutes. Stir in garlic, ginger, and crushed red pepper; cook for 1 minute. Add broth, orange juice, and teriyaki sauce; bring to boiling, scraping pan bottom. Return beef to pan, cover and simmer over low heat 45 to 60 minutes or until beef is tender. Add bok choy leaves the last 5 minutes of cooking. Serve with hot cooked rice, if desired.

FOR 16 SERVINGS Use a 6- to 8-qt. Dutch oven.

PER SERVING *314 cal., 19 g fat (7 g sat. fat), 99 mg chol., 665 mg sodium, 11 g carb., 1 g fiber, 25 g pro.*

PREP 30 minutes
COOK 45 minutes

8 servings	ingredients	16 servings
2 lb.	boneless beef chuck roast, cut into 1-inch pieces	4 lb.
1 Tbsp.	Chinese five-spice powder	2 Tbsp.
½ tsp.	salt	1 tsp.
1 Tbsp.	canola oil	2 Tbsp.
4 oz.	fresh shiitake mushrooms, stemmed and sliced	8 oz.
12 oz.	bok choy, sliced crosswise, white and green portions separated	24 oz.
3	cloves garlic, minced	6
1 Tbsp.	grated fresh ginger	2 Tbsp.
½ tsp.	crushed red pepper	1 tsp.
2 cups	lower-sodium beef broth	4 cups
1 cup	orange juice	2 cups
½ cup	reduced-sodium teriyaki sauce	1 cup
	Hot cooked rice (optional)	

Italian Roast Beef Slider Melts

Perfect for a party or a quick weeknight meal, these tasty sliders are always a hit. Use either mild or hot giardiniera, depending on your personal taste.

1. Preheat oven to 350°F. Arrange roll bottoms in a 9×13-inch baking pan. Layer with roast beef, pickled mixed vegetables, and provolone cheese. Spread cut sides of roll tops with cream cheese; place on sandwiches.

2. In a bowl combine the remaining ingredients. Drizzle over rolls. Cover pan with foil.

3. Bake 15 minutes. Remove foil; bake 10 to 15 minutes more or until cheese is melted and roll tops are lightly browned.

FOR 24 SERVINGS Use two 9×13-inch baking pans.

TO MAKE AHEAD Assemble the sandwiches. Do not drizzle with olive oil mixture. Cover and refrigerate up to 8 hours. Drizzle and bake as directed.

PER SERVING *362 cal., 16 g fat (7 g sat. fat), 51 mg chol., 881 mg sodium, 35 g carb., 1 g fiber, 19 g pro.*

PREP 20 minutes
BAKE 25 minutes at 350°F

12 servings	ingredients	24 servings
12	3-inch pretzel or sourdough rolls	24
12 oz.	thinly sliced deli-style roast beef	24 oz.
1½ cups	chopped pickled mixed vegetables (giardiniera)	3 cups
6 oz.	thinly sliced provolone or mozzarella cheese	12 oz.
one 8-oz. tub	cream cheese spread with garden vegetables	two 8-oz. tubs
¼ cup	olive oil	½ cup
2	cloves garlic, minced	4
1 tsp.	dried Italian seasoning, crushed	2 tsp.
½ tsp.	crushed red pepper	1 tsp.

Tacos in Pasta Shells

PREP 40 minutes
BAKE 30 minutes at 350°F

4 servings	ingredients	8 servings
12	dried jumbo macaroni shells	24
¾ lb.	extra-lean ground beef	1½ lb.
1¼ cups	salsa	2½ cups
2 oz.	reduced-fat cream cheese (neufchatel), cut up	4 oz.
½ tsp.	chili powder	1 tsp.
½ cup	shredded reduced-fat cheddar cheese	1 cup
	Chopped tomato (optional)	
	Sliced pitted ripe olives (optional)	

Two favorite flavor profiles—Italian and Mexican—come together in this family-friendly dish. Take it to a potluck and it will disappear in an instant.

1. Cook shells according to package directions; drain. Rinse with cold water; drain again.

2. Meanwhile, preheat oven to 350°F. In an extra-large skillet cook ground beef over medium-high heat until browned. Drain off fat. Stir in ½ cup of the salsa, the cream cheese, and chili powder. Remove from heat; cool slightly. Fill cooked shells with meat mixture.

3. Spread ½ cup of the salsa in an 8×8-inch baking dish. Arrange filled shells in dish; top with remaining salsa.

4. Bake, covered, 15 minutes. Sprinkle with cheddar cheese. Bake, uncovered, 15 minutes more or until heated through. If desired, sprinkle with tomato and olives.

FOR 8 SERVINGS Use a 9×13-inch baking pan. In Step 2, use 1 cup of the salsa. In Step 3, use 1 cup of the salsa.

PER SERVING *307 cal., 11 g fat (5 g sat. fat), 67 mg chol., 710 mg sodium, 28 g carb., 3 g fiber, 25 g pro.*

Mini Meat Loaves with Potatoes and Beans

This fun twist on the classic diner blue-plate special of meat loaf, potatoes, and green beans is made in a single pan—making cleanup a snap.

1. Preheat oven to 350°F. Line a 9×13-inch baking pan with foil. In a bowl stir together the first seven ingredients (through garlic) and half the mustard. Add beef; mix well. Divide into four equal portions and shape into round loaves. Place on one side of the pan. In a bowl stir together the ¼ cup ketchup, brown sugar, and remaining mustard. Spread over meat loaves.

2. In another bowl combine the next five ingredients (through black pepper); toss to coat. Arrange in opposite half of pan.

3. Bake, uncovered, 40 to 45 minutes or until meat loaves are done (160°F) and vegetables are tender, adding green beans to the potatoes after 20 minutes.

FOR 8 SERVINGS Use two 9×13-inch baking pans. In Step 1, use ½ cup ketchup.

PER SERVING *345 cal., 12 g fat (4 g sat. fat), 118 mg chol., 512 mg sodium, 31 g carb., 4 g fiber, 29 g pro.*

PREP 30 minutes
BAKE 40 minutes at 350°F

4 servings	ingredients	8 servings
1	egg, lightly beaten	2
3 Tbsp.	fine dry bread crumbs	6 Tbsp.
¼ cup	shredded carrot	½ cup
¼ cup	finely chopped onion	½ cup
1 Tbsp.	ketchup	2 Tbsp.
1 tsp.	Worcestershire sauce	2 tsp.
1	clove garlic, minced	2
2 tsp.	yellow mustard	4 tsp.
1 lb.	extra-lean ground beef	2 lb.
¼ cup	ketchup	½ cup
2 Tbsp.	packed brown sugar	¼ cup
8 oz.	fingerling potatoes	16 oz.
2 tsp.	olive oil	4 tsp.
1 tsp.	dried thyme	2 tsp.
¼ tsp.	salt	½ tsp.
¼ tsp.	black pepper	½ tsp.
8 oz.	fresh green beans, trimmed	16 oz.

Pork Chops with Roasted Vegetables and Balsamic Drizzle

This dish features a delicious and healthful combination of root vegetables—sweet potatoes, Brussels sprouts, and parsnip. It's quick and easy enough for a weeknight but perfectly appropriate for a casual fall dinner with friends.

PREP 25 minutes
ROAST 35 minutes at 425°F

4 servings	ingredients	8 servings
¼ cup	balsamic vinegar	½ cup
1 Tbsp.	tomato paste	2 Tbsp.
1 Tbsp.	honey	2 Tbsp.
¾ tsp.	smoked black pepper	1½ tsp.
½ tsp.	salt	1 tsp.
1	large sweet potato, cut into ½-inch wedges	2
8 oz.	Brussels sprouts, trimmed and halved	16 oz.
1	medium parsnip, cut into ½-inch slices	2
3 Tbsp.	olive oil	6 Tbsp.
four 4- to 5-oz.	1-inch-thick boneless pork loin chops, trimmed	eight 4- to 5-oz.
1 tsp.	dried herbes de Provence	2 tsp.
½ cup	crumbled goat cheese (chèvre)	1 cup

1. Preheat oven to 425°F. In a small bowl combine vinegar, tomato paste, honey, ¼ tsp. of the pepper, and half the salt.

2. In a 9×13-inch baking dish combine sweet potato, Brussels sprouts, and parsnip. Drizzle with 2 Tbsp. of the oil; toss to coat. Roast, uncovered, 25 minutes.

3. Meanwhile, sprinkle chops with herbes de Provence and remaining pepper and salt. In a large skillet heat remaining oil over medium-high heat. Add chops; cook 2 minutes or until browned, turning once.

4. Place chops on vegetables. Roast 10 to 15 minutes or until a thermometer inserted in center of chops registers 145°F and vegetables are tender. Sprinkle with cheese and drizzle with balsamic.

FOR 8 SERVINGS In Step 1, use ½ tsp. of the smoked black pepper. In Step 2, use two 9×13-inch baking dishes drizzle vegetables with 4 Tbsp. of the oil.

PER SERVING *442 cal., 19 g fat (6 g sat. fat), 89 mg chol., 516 mg sodium, 36 g carb., 7 g fiber, 32 g pro.*

Ginger-Soy Pork Chops on Greens

You can afford to indulge in dessert after eating this light and healthful meal—just 259 calories and 8 grams of fat per serving.

START TO FINISH 40 minutes

4 servings	ingredients	8 servings
four 6- to 7-oz.	bone-in pork chops, trimmed (about ½ inch thick)	eight 6- to 7-oz.
¼ cup	reduced-sodium soy sauce	½ cup
3 Tbsp.	lime juice	6 Tbsp.
2 Tbsp.	sugar	¼ cup
1 Tbsp.	canola oil	2 Tbsp.
1 Tbsp.	cider vinegar	2 Tbsp.
2 tsp.	grated fresh ginger	4 tsp.
¼ tsp.	crushed red pepper	½ tsp.
4 cups	mixed spring greens	8 cups
½ cup	chopped fresh cilantro	1 cup

1. Place chops in a 9×13-inch baking dish. For marinade, in a bowl whisk together the next seven ingredients (through crushed red pepper). Spoon 2 Tbsp. of the marinade over chops and turn to coat. Cover dish with plastic wrap and let stand at room temperature 20 minutes, turning occasionally.

2. Place the remaining marinade in a small saucepan. Bring to boiling. Boil gently 1 to 2 minutes or until reduced to ¼ cup.

3. Grill chops, covered, directly over medium heat 3 minutes per side or until browned and a thermometer inserted in centers of chops registers 145°F, turning once.

4. Serve chops with greens; drizzle with reduced marinade. Sprinkle with cilantro.

FOR 8 SERVINGS Use two 9×13-inch baking dishes. In Step 1, spoon ¼ cup of the marinade over chops. In Step 2, reduce remaining marinade to ½ cup.

PER SERVING *259 cal., 8 g fat (2 g sat. fat), 93 mg chol., 614 mg sodium, 11 g carb., 1 g fiber, 33 g pro.*

Spicy Skillet Pork Chops

A quick sear gives these chops a nicely browned and caramelized crust. Cooking them through in a covered pan with the vegetables keeps them tender and juicy.

1. In a bowl combine the first five ingredients (through hot pepper sauce).

2. Trim fat from chops. Sprinkle both sides with chili powder. In a large skillet heat oil over medium-high heat. Add chops; cook 4 minutes or until browned, turning once. Remove chops, reserving drippings in skillet.

3. Add onions to reserved drippings; cook and stir over medium heat 3 minutes. Stir in corn mixture; top with chops. Bring to boiling; reduce heat. Simmer, covered, 10 to 12 minutes or until a thermometer inserted in centers of chops registers 145°F.

4. If desired, sprinkle chops with cilantro. Serve with hot cooked rice.

PER SERVING *396 cal., 10 g fat (2 g sat. fat), 107 mg chol., 369 mg sodium, 32 g carb., 2 g fiber, 42 g pro.*

PREP 35 minutes
COOK 10 minutes

4 servings	ingredients	8 servings
1½ cups	frozen whole kernel corn	3 cups
one 10-oz. can	diced tomatoes and green chiles, undrained	two 10-oz. cans
2	cloves garlic, minced	4
½ tsp.	ground cumin	1 tsp.
¼ tsp.	bottled hot pepper sauce	½ tsp.
4	boneless pork loin chops, cut ¾ inch thick	8
½ tsp.	chili powder	1 tsp.
1½ tsp.	vegetable oil	1 Tbsp.
1	medium onions, cut into thin wedges	2
	Fresh cilantro (optional)	
	Hot cooked rice	

Pork Cassoulet

Traditional cassoulet is a very rich, time-consuming French dish. This quicker, lighter version can be enjoyed any day of the week—and is just as warming on a cold winter night.

PREP 25 minutes
BAKE 25 minutes at 350°F

6 servings	ingredients	12 servings
1 Tbsp.	olive oil	2 Tbsp.
½ cup	chopped onion	1 cup
½ cup	chopped carrot	1 cup
½ cup	thinly sliced celery	1 cup
1 lb.	pork tenderloin, trimmed and cut into 1-inch pieces	2 lb.
6 oz.	smoked turkey sausage, thinly sliced	12 oz.
two 15-oz. cans	no-salt-added Great Northern beans, rinsed and drained	four 15-oz. cans
⅔ cup	chopped roma tomatoes	1⅓ cups
½ cup	reduced-sodium chicken broth	1 cup
2 Tbsp.	tomato paste	4 Tbsp.
1 tsp.	dried Italian seasoning, crushed	2 tsp.
2 Tbsp.	snipped fresh Italian parsley	¼ cup
	Salt and black pepper	

1. Preheat oven to 350°F. In a large skillet heat oil over medium heat. Add onion, carrot, and celery; cook 5 minutes, stirring occasionally. Add pork and sausage; cook 5 minutes more or until browned.

2. In a bowl mash half the beans. Stir in remaining beans, tomatoes, broth, tomato paste, and Italian seasoning. Stir into meat mixture. Transfer to an 8×8-inch baking dish.

3. Bake, covered, 25 minutes or until pork is tender. Sprinkle with parsley. Season to taste with salt and pepper

FOR 12 SERVINGS Use a 9×13-inch baking pan.

PER SERVING *278 cal., 7 g fat (2 g sat. fat), 64 mg chol., 530 mg sodium, 26 g carb., 9 g fiber, 26 g pro.*

Pork and Potatoes with Minted Yogurt

A savory blend of cumin, chili powder, and garlic powder flavors both the pork and potatoes in this easy dish. Serve it with a crisp green salad or slices of ripe tomato dressed with olive oil and a little salt and black pepper.

1. Preheat oven to 425°F. Line a 15×10-inch baking pan with foil. In a bowl combine cumin, chili powder, salt, and garlic powder. Set aside 1 teaspoon of the spice mixture. Place tenderloin in the prepared pan. Brush with half the oil. Sprinkle pork with remaining spice mixture, rubbing in with your fingers. Arrange potatoes around pork in pan. Drizzle potatoes with remaining oil and sprinkle with reserved spice mixture; toss to coat. Roast 25 to 30 minutes or until thermometer inserted in centers of chops registers 145°F and potatoes are tender. Cover and let stand 3 minutes.

2. Meanwhile, for Minted Yogurt, remove 1 tsp. zest and squeeze 1 tsp. juice from lemon. In a bowl stir together yogurt, cucumber, mint, lemon zest, and lemon juice. Season to taste with salt and black pepper. Serve sliced pork with potatoes and Minted Yogurt.

FOR 12 SERVINGS Use two 15×10-inch baking pans. In Step 1, reserve 2 tsp. spice mixture. In Step 2 remove 2 tsp. zest and squeeze 2 tsp. juice from lemon.

PER SERVING *321 cal., 11 g fat (2 g sat. fat), 77 mg chol., 736 mg sodium, 23 g carb., 4 g fiber, 32 g pro.*

PREP 25 minutes
ROAST 25 minutes at 425°F
STAND 3 minutes

4 servings	ingredients	8 servings
2 tsp.	ground cumin	4 tsp.
2 tsp.	chili powder	4 tsp.
1 tsp.	salt	2 tsp.
½ tsp.	garlic powder	1 tsp.
one 1-lb.	pork tenderloin	two 1-lb.
2 Tbsp.	canola oil	¼ cup
1 lb.	tiny yellow new potatoes, cut into 1-inch chunks	2 lb.
1	lemon	1
1 cup	plain Greek yogurt	2 cups
½ cup	chopped cucumber	1 cup
½ cup	chopped fresh mint	1 cup
	Salt and black pepper	

Pork and Squash Enchiladas

Cooked and pureed winter squash adds a touch of sweetness—and good nutrition—to the filling for these enchiladas.

1. Preheat oven to 350°F. In a large nonstick skillet heat half the oil over medium heat. Add pork; cook and stir 1 minute. Add onion slices and additional oil if necessary. Add tomatoes and chili powder; cook and stir 2 minutes.

2. Pour ⅓ cup enchilada sauce into a 9×13-inch baking dish; tilt dish to coat bottom. Stack tortillas and wrap in damp paper towels. Microwave 40 seconds or until warm and soft. Top each tortilla with a slightly rounded tablespoon of the squash, about ¼ cup of the pork mixture, and 1 Tbsp. of the cheese. Roll up; place, seam sides down, in the prepared baking dish. Pour remaining sauce over enchiladas and sprinkle with remaining cheese.

3. Bake, covered, 25 minutes or until heated through and cheese melts. If desired, serve with sour cream, salsa, and/or cilantro.

FOR 12 SERVINGS Use two 9×13-inch baking pans.

PER SERVING *397 cal., 18 g fat (8 g sat. fat), 85 mg chol., 893 mg sodium, 31 g carb., 5 g fiber, 29 g pro.*

PREP 25 minutes
BAKE 25 minutes at 350°F

6 servings	ingredients	12 servings
1 Tbsp.	olive oil	2 Tbsp.
1 lb.	pork tenderloin, cut into small pieces	2 lb.
1	small onion, halved lengthwise and thinly sliced	2
one 10-oz. can	diced tomatoes and green chiles, drained	two 10-oz. cans
1 tsp.	chili powder	2 tsp.
one 14-oz. can	mild enchilada sauce	two 14-oz. cans
12	6-inch corn tortillas	24
one 12-oz. pkg.	frozen cooked winter squash, thawed	two 12-oz. pkg.
2 cups	shredded Mexican-style four-cheese blend	4 cups
	Light sour cream, salsa, and/or cilantro leaves (optional)	

Spicy Asian Pork Cabbage Rolls

This twist on traditional stuffed cabbage is flavored with shiitake mushrooms, cilantro, pickled ginger, soy sauce, and toasted sesame oil.

6 servings	ingredients	12 servings
	Nonstick cooking spray	
½	large head green cabbage	1
½ tsp.	salt	1 tsp.
1	egg, lightly beaten	1
½ cup	cooked brown rice	1 cup
½ cup	finely chopped stemmed fresh shiitake mushrooms	1 cup
¼ cup	frozen edamame, thawed	½ cup
¼ cup	snipped fresh cilantro	½ cup
2 Tbsp.	finely chopped carrot	⅓ cup
1 Tbsp.	finely chopped green onion	2 Tbsp.
1 Tbsp.	chopped pickled ginger	2 Tbsp.
1 Tbsp.	reduced-sodium soy sauce	2 Tbsp.
1 tsp.	toasted sesame oil	2 tsp.
4 oz.	lean ground pork	8 oz.
	Asian Braising Sauce	
	Fresh cilantro sprigs (optional)	

1. Lightly coat an 8×8-inch baking dish with cooking spray. Carefully remove 6 outer leaves from cabbage. Finely chop enough remaining cabbage to measure 3 cups. Transfer chopped cabbage to a colander; sprinkle with salt. Set colander in a sink and let stand 30 minutes. Meanwhile, trim the thick vein on the back of each cabbage leaf even with the rest of the leaf. Immerse leaves, four at a time, into boiling water 2 to 3 minutes or just until limp.

2. Preheat oven to 400°F. In a bowl combine the next 10 ingredients (through sesame oil). Add ground pork; mix well. Squeeze excess water from chopped cabbage; stir cabbage into pork mixture.

3. Place about ½ cup of the pork mixture on the stem end of each cabbage leaf. Fold in sides and roll up leaf to enclose filling. Place cabbage rolls, seam sides down, in the prepared baking dish. Pour Asian Braising Sauce over cabbage rolls.

4. Bake, covered, 20 minutes. Uncover and bake 15 to 20 minutes more or until done (165°F). If desired, top each serving with fresh cilantro sprigs.

ASIAN BRAISING SAUCE In a bowl combine half an 8-oz. can tomato sauce; 4½ tsp. hoisin sauce; 1 Tbsp. each rice vinegar, honey, tomato paste, reduced-sodium soy sauce, and oyster sauce; and ¼ tsp. sriracha sauce.

FOR 12 SERVINGS Use a 9×13-inch baking dish. In Step 1, remove 12 outer leaves from cabbage. Finely chop enough remaining cabbage to measure 6 cups. Use one 8-oz. can tomato sauce; 3 Tbsp. hoisin sauce; 2 Tbsp. each rice vinegar, honey, tomato paste, reduced-sodium soy sauce, and oyster sauce; and ½ tsp. sriracha sauce.

PER SERVING *248 cal., 5 g fat (1 g sat. fat), 54 mg chol., 1,378 mg sodium, 37 g carb., 8 g fiber, 16 g pro.*

Roasted Sausage with Mushrooms, Squash, and Polenta

This rustically elegant one-pan meal is inspired by northern Italian cooking. Serve it with a glass of chilled Pinot Grigio if you like.

1. Preheat oven to 425°F. In a 15×10-inch baking pan combine polenta, mushrooms, and squash. Drizzle with oil and sprinkle with salt and pepper.

2. Prick each sausage a few times with a fork. Place in pan with vegetables. Sprinkle with rosemary.

3. Roast 30 minutes or until sausages are done (160°F), stirring once. If desired, top with additional rosemary.

FOR 12 SERVINGS Use two 15×10-inch baking pans.

PER SERVING *403 cal., 31 g fat (9 g sat. fat), 57 mg chol., 850 mg sodium, 18 g carb., 2 g fiber, 14 g pro.*

PREP 15 minutes
ROAST 30 minutes at 425°F

6 servings	ingredients	12 servings
one 16-oz. tube	refrigerated cooked polenta, cut into ½-inch slices and halved	two 16-oz. tubes
2 cups	sliced fresh cremini mushrooms	4 cups
2 cups	cubed, peeled butternut squash	4 cups
3 Tbsp.	olive oil	6 Tbsp.
	Salt and black pepper	
1 lb.	uncooked mild Italian sausage links	2 lb.
1 tsp.	snipped fresh rosemary	2 tsp.

Sweet Potato-Chorizo Lasagna

The combination of sweet and spicy flavors in this unusual lasagna is irresistible. It's not super-cheesy like traditional lasagna, but the pureed sweet potato gives it a distinctive creaminess.

1. Preheat oven to 375°F. For sweet potato sauce, place sweet potatoes on a foil-lined baking sheet. Bake 60 minutes or until tender when pierced with a fork. Remove from oven; cool. Peel; discard skin. Transfer sweet potatoes to a food processor. Add milk, lime juice, and cumin. Cover; process until smooth.

2. In a large skillet cook chorizo over medium heat for 5 minutes or until done (160°F). Remove from heat. Drain off fat.

3. Meanwhile, cook noodles according to package directions until tender but still firm (al dente). Drain; rinse with cold water. Drain well.

4. Drizzle bottom of an 9×13-inch baking dish with olive oil. Arrange three of the noodles in a single layer over oil. Spread one-fourth of sweet potato sauce over noodles. Top with one-fourth each of the chorizo, green onions, cilantro, and cheddar cheese. Repeat layers three more times. Cover with parchment brushed with olive oil, coated side down; seal tightly with foil.

5. Bake 40 minutes. Uncover; bake 5 minutes more or until cheese is golden brown and sauce is bubbly. Let stand 20 minutes before serving.

FOR 16 SERVINGS Use two 9×13-inch baking pans. In Step 4, arrange six of the noodles in a single layer over oil.

PER SERVING *684 cal., 41 g fat (17 g sat. fat), 96 mg chol., 1,184 mg sodium, 46 g carb., 4 g fiber, 32 g pro.*

PREP 30 minutes
BAKE 1 hour 45 minutes at 375°F
STAND 20 minutes

8 servings	ingredients	16 servings
2 lb.	sweet potatoes	4 lb.
1¼ cups	milk	2½ cups
2 Tbsp.	lime juice	¼ cup
2 tsp.	ground cumin	4 tsp.
three 7.5-oz. links	uncooked chorizo sausage	six 7.5-oz. links
12	dried lasagna noodles	24
	Olive oil	
¼ cup	thinly sliced green onions	½ cup
¼ cup	chopped fresh cilantro	½ cup
1½ cups	shredded sharp white cheddar cheese	3 cups

Zoodle Pizza Casserole

Go low-carb with this combination of pizza and lasagna that calls for spiralized zucchini instead of pasta. Kids will love it!

PREP 30 minutes
STAND 15 minutes
BAKE 25 minutes at 400°F

8 servings	ingredients	16 servings
	Nonstick cooking spray	
two 8- to 9-oz.	zucchini	four 8- to 9-oz.
¾ tsp.	kosher salt	1½ tsp.
1	eggs, lightly beaten	2
1 cup	shredded mozzarella cheese	2 cups
2 Tbsp.	grated Parmesan cheese	¼ cup
2 Tbsp.	all-purpose flour	¼ cup
1 Tbsp.	cornmeal	2 Tbsp.
half 8-oz. can	pizza sauce	one 8-oz. can
¼ cup	miniature sliced pepperoni	½ cup

1. Preheat oven to 400°F. Coat an 8×8-inch baking dish with cooking spray. Using a vegetable spiralizer, julienne cutter, or mandoline, cut zucchini into long, thin noodles (zoodles). Place in a colander set in a sink and sprinkle with salt; toss gently. Let stand 15 minutes. Pat dry with paper towels.

2. In a bowl combine eggs, one-fourth of the mozzarella cheese, the Parmesan cheese, flour, and cornmeal. Stir in zoodles. Transfer to prepared dish.

3. Bake, uncovered, 10 minutes or until set and no excess liquid remains. Spread pizza sauce over zoodle mixture. Top with remaining mozzarella cheese and the pepperoni. Bake 15 to 20 minutes more or until cheese is lightly browned.

FOR 8 SERVINGS Use a 9×13-inch baking pan.

PER SERVING *191 cal., 10 g fat (5 g sat. fat), 75 mg chol., 678 mg sodium, 12 g carb., 2 g fiber, 13 g pro.*

Creamy Alfredo with Bacon and Peas

This dish will be a hit with every person who pulls up a chair at your table. Who can resist pasta, bacon, cream, and cheese? Just a small amount of cream gives it incredibly rich texture.

1. In a large deep skillet cook the chopped bacon over medium heat until crisp. Add garlic; cook and stir 30 seconds more. Drain off fat. Stir in pasta, broth, the water, salt, and pepper.

2. Bring to boiling; reduce heat. Simmer, covered, 12 to 15 minutes or until pasta is tender but still firm, stirring once. Stir in peas, cream, and cheese. Cook 2 minutes or until heated through. If desired, sprinkle with crumbled bacon.

PER SERVING *378 cal., 13 g fat (6 g sat. fat), 37 mg chol., 1,043 mg sodium, 49 g carb., 3 g fiber, 16 g pro.*

START TO FINISH 35 minutes

4 servings	ingredients	8 servings
4	thick slices bacon, coarsely chopped	8
2	cloves garlic, minced	4
8 oz.	dried penne, rotini, or rigatoni pasta	16 oz.
one 14.5-oz. can	chicken broth	two 14.5-oz. cans
1 cup	water	2 cups
½ tsp.	salt	1 tsp.
¼ tsp.	black pepper	½ tsp.
1 cup	frozen peas	2 cups
¼ to ⅓ cup	heavy cream	½ to ⅔ cup
¼ cup	grated Parmesan cheese	½ cup
	Crumbled, crisp-cooked bacon (optional)	

Egg Baguette Bake

This egg-and-sausage-stuffed bread is suited to either brunch or supper. Serve it with fruit in the morning and a green salad in the evening.

1. Preheat oven to 350°F. Line a 9×13-inch baking pan with parchment paper. Using a serrated knife, cut a wedge into the top of loaf, cutting to about 1 inch from each side. Use a spoon or fingers to remove inside of loaf, leaving about ¾-inch shell. Arrange bread shell in prepared baking pan.

2. Remove casing from sausage if present. In a large skillet crumble and cook sausage with sweet pepper 8 minutes or just until sausage is cooked and pepper is tender, stirring in green onions the last 1 minute of cooking. Remove from heat; drain off fat.

3. In a large bowl combine eggs, cream, basil, and salt. Stir in sausage and peppers and ½ cup of the cheese.

4. Carefully pour egg filling into bread shell. Sprinkle with remaining cheese. Bake, uncovered, 35 to 40 minutes or until eggs are done (160°F). Let stand 5 minutes. Using a serrated knife, carefully cut loaf into slices.

FOR 10 SERVINGS Use a 15×10-inch baking pan. In Step 3, use 1 cup of the cheese.

PER SERVING *490 cal., 23 g fat (11 g sat. fat), 245 mg chol., 977 mg sodium, 45 g carb., 0 g fiber, 20 g pro.*

PREP 30 minutes
BAKE 35 minutes at 350°F
STAND 5 minutes

5 servings	ingredients	10 servings
one 1-lb.	Italian or French baguettes (12×4-inch)	two 1-lb.
4 oz.	sweet or mild Italian sausage	8 oz.
⅓ cup	chopped red or yellow sweet pepper	⅔ cup
¼ cup	sliced green onions	½ cup
5	eggs, lightly beaten	10
⅓ cup	heavy cream or half-and-half	⅔ cup
½ cup	snipped fresh basil	1 cup
¼ tsp.	salt	½ tsp.
¾ cup	shredded Fontina, mozzarella, or provolone cheese	1½ cups

Roasted Pear-Ham Melts

A slather of red pepper jelly adds sweetness and a little heat to this toasty sandwich. It calls for white cheddar, but muenster, Havarti, or Gouda cheese would be tasty, too.

PREP 20 minutes
BAKE 20 minutes at 425°F

4 servings	ingredients	8 servings
4	pears, cored and cut lengthwise into ½-inch slices	8
2 Tbsp.	olive oil	¼ cup
8	½-inch slices white bread	16
½ cup	red pepper jelly	1 cup
8 oz.	thinly sliced ham	16 oz.
4	slices white cheddar cheese	8

1. Preheat oven to 425°F. In a 15×10-inch baking pan toss pear slices with oil. Roast 20 to 25 minutes or until very tender. Cool slightly.

2. Spread one side of bread slices with pepper jelly. Layer half the bread slices with ham, roasted pear slices, and cheese. Top with remaining bread slices, spread sides down. Brush both sides of each sandwich with additional olive oil.

3. Heat a large skillet or griddle over medium heat. Cook sandwiches 2 to 3 minutes or until bottoms are golden and cheese is melted, turning once.

PER SERVING *709 cal., 22 g fat (7 g sat. fat), 54 mg chol., 1,286 mg sodium, 106 g carb., 9 g fiber, 24 g pro.*

Smoky Pizza Melts

When you need to serve a crowd something everyone will love, these gooey sandwiches are the perfect choice. To make them ahead, assemble, cover, and refrigerate until 30 minutes before serving. Then just drizzle and bake.

PREP 35 minutes
BAKE 25 minutes 350°F

12 servings	ingredients	24 servings
½ cup	grated Parmesan cheese	1 cup
¼ cup	olive oil	½ cup
1	clove minced garlic	2
2 Tbsp.	melted butter	¼ cup
1 tsp.	dried oregano, crushed	2 tsp.
½ tsp.	crushed red pepper	1 tsp.
12	ciabatta rolls, split	24
one 12-oz. jar	marinated artichoke hearts, drained and chopped	two 12-oz. jars
1 cup	thinly sliced green sweet pepper	2 cups
4 oz.	sliced pepperoni	8 oz.
one 2.25-oz. can	sliced pitted ripe olives, drained	two 2.25-oz. cans
6 oz.	shredded smoked mozzarella cheese	12 oz.
one 8 oz. can	pizza sauce	two 8 oz. cans

1. Preheat oven to 350°F. For the drizzle, in a bowl combine the first six ingredients (through crushed red pepper).

2. Arrange bottoms of rolls in a 9×13-inch baking pan. For each sandwich, on roll bottoms layer chopped artichoke hearts, sweet pepper strips, pepperoni, and olives. Top with mozzarella cheese. Spread cut sides of roll tops with pizza sauce, then place on sandwiches. Spoon drizzle over sandwiches.

3. Cover pan with foil. Bake 15 minutes. Remove foil; bake 10 to 15 minutes more or until cheese is melted and roll tops are lightly browned.

FOR 24 SERVINGS Use two 9×13-inch baking pans.

PER SERVING *317 cal., 16 g fat (6 g sat. fat), 28 mg chol., 963 mg sodium, 32 g carb., 2 g fiber, 12 g pro.*

Cajun Sausage-Potato Soup

Don't skip the sliced green onions on top! They add a fresh crunch and flavor to the rich and creamy soup.

1. In a 4-qt. Dutch oven combine first six ingredients (through Cajun seasoning). Bring to boiling; reduce heat. Simmer 10 minutes or until potatoes are tender, stirring occasionally.

2. Before serving, stir in cream. If desired, top servings with green onions.

FOR 12 SERVINGS Use a 6- to 8-qt. Dutch oven.

PER SERVING *363 cal., 26 g fat (11 g sat. fat), 67 mg chol., 1,113 mg sodium, 20 g carb., 2 g fiber, 12 g pro.*

PREP 20 minutes
COOK 10 minutes

6 servings	ingredients	12 servings
4 cups	frozen diced hash brown potatoes with onions and peppers	8 cups
one 14.5-oz. can	reduced-sodium chicken broth	two 14.5-oz. cans
one 13.5- to 14-oz. pkg.	cooked andouille or other smoked sausage, chopped	two 13.5- to 14-oz. pkg.
1 cup	water	2 cups
one 10.75-oz. can	condensed cream of celery soup	two 10.75-oz. cans
2 tsp.	Cajun seasoning	4 tsp.
½ cup	heavy cream	1 cup
	Sliced green onions (optional)	

Pork and Wild Rice Soup

Dried mushrooms give this soup incredibly rich flavor—and it couldn't be simpler to make. Just combine everything in a pot, simmer for 10 minutes, and dinner is done!

1. In a 4-qt. Dutch oven combine all ingredients. Bring just to boiling; reduce heat. Simmer, covered, 10 minutes, stirring occasionally. If desired, top servings with additional fresh sage.

FOR 12 SERVINGS Use a 6- to 8-qt. Dutch oven.

TIP If desired, for 6 servings, use 1 tsp. dried sage, crushed, for the fresh sage. For 12 servings, use 2 tsp. dried sage for the fresh sage.

PER SERVING *219 cal., 5 g fat (2 g sat. fat), 38 mg chol., 1,065 mg sodium, 24 g carb., 1 g fiber, 18 g pro.*

PREP 15 minutes
COOK 10 minutes

6 servings	ingredients	12 servings
one 32-oz. carton	reduced-sodium chicken broth	two 32-oz. cartons
two 8.8-oz. pouches	cooked long grain and wild rice	four 8.8-oz. pouches
one 15-oz. pkg.	refrigerated cooked pork roast au jus, broken into chunks	two 15-oz. pkg.
½ oz.	dried porcini or oyster mushrooms, broken and rinsed	1 oz.
1 Tbsp.	snipped fresh sage	2 Tbsp.

CHAPTER 4

Seafood

Fresh and light seafood is a healthful addition to your diet—and it adapts to many flavor profiles—including Asian, Mexican, Italian, and classic American.

108 Tilapia Pasta

110 Parmesan-Crusted Cod with Garlicky Summer Squash

111 Basil Halibut with Jalapeño Butter

113 Chipotle-Cilantro Tilapia

114 Salmon Vera Cruz

115 Lemon-Herb Roasted Salmon with Broccoli and Tomatoes

116 Salmon with Tomatoes and Olives

118 Salmon with Roasted Tomatoes and Shallots

119 Salmon Patties with Parsley Mayo

120 Creamy Tuna-Noodle Toss

121 Lemony Tuna Salad

123 Tuna-Noodle Casserole

124 Grilled Shrimp in Coconut Milk Sauce

125 Baked Shrimp and Rice

127 Spicy Shrimp with Cabbage-Noodle Slaw

129 Basil Shrimp Chowder

130 Thai Coconut and Basmati Rice with Seared Scallops

113

118

127

Tilapia Pasta

This dish—flavored with fennel, garlic, capers, and tomatoes—is inspired by the fresh seafood pastas popular at the trattorias at seaside villages in Italy.

START TO FINISH 40 minutes

6 servings	ingredients	12 servings
12 oz.	fresh or frozen tilapia fillets	24 oz.
8 oz.	dried linguine	16 oz.
⅛ tsp.	salt	¼ tsp.
⅛ tsp.	black pepper	¼ tsp.
2 Tbsp.	olive oil	¼ cup
1 cup	finely chopped onion	2 cups
one 8-oz.	fennel bulb, trimmed, cored, and chopped	two 8-oz.
1 Tbsp.	minced fresh garlic	2 Tbsp.
1 Tbsp.	capers	2 Tbsp.
1 tsp.	dried Italian seasoning, crushed	2 tsp.
one 14.5-oz. can	diced tomatoes, undrained	two 14.5-oz. cans
one 8-oz. can	tomato sauce	two 8-oz. cans
1 Tbsp.	snipped fresh Italian parsley	2 Tbsp.

1. Thaw fish, if frozen. Rinse fish; pat dry with paper towels. Cook pasta according to package directions. Drain, reserving ¼ cup of the cooking water. Meanwhile, season fish with salt and pepper. In an extra-large skillet heat half the oil over medium-high heat. Add fish; cook 6 minutes or until fish flakes easily. Remove fish.

2. Add the remaining oil to skillet. Add onion and fennel. Cook and stir 5 minutes or until tender. Stir in garlic, capers, and Italian seasoning; cook 1 minute more. Stir in tomatoes, tomato sauce, and the reserved pasta water. Bring to boiling. Boil gently, uncovered, 8 minutes, stirring occasionally. Remove from heat. Stir in the pasta and fish, breaking up fish slightly. Sprinkle with parsley.

FOR 12 SERVINGS In Step 1, reserve ½ cup cooking water.

PER SERVING *283 cal., 6 g fat (1 g sat. fat), 28 mg chol., 458 mg sodium, 39 g carb., 4 g fiber, 18 g pro.*

Parmesan-Crusted Cod with Garlicky Summer Squash

Panko bread crumbs—larger and airier than traditional bread crumbs—create an especially crunchy crust on the cod. The crisp exterior yields to the tender, buttery texture of the fish. Serve with wedges of lemon for squeezing if you like.

1. Thaw fish, if frozen. Preheat oven to 350°F. In a 15×10-inch baking pan combine squash and garlic. Drizzle with half the oil. Rinse fish; pat dry. Place in pan with squash. Sprinkle fish and squash lightly with salt and pepper.

2. In a bowl combine panko, cheese, parsley, and salt. Drizzle with remaining oil; toss to coat. Sprinkle on top of fish; press lightly. If desired, sprinkle with additional parsley.

PER SERVING *297 cal., 16 g fat (3 g sat. fat), 65 mg chol., 409 mg sodium, 8 g carb., 2 g fiber, 29 g pro.*

PREP 20 minutes
BAKE 20 minutes at 350°F

4 servings	ingredients	8 servings
four 5- to 6-oz.	fresh or frozen skinless cod fillets	eight 5- to 6-oz.
4	small zucchini and/or yellow summer squash, cut into ¾-inch pieces	8
2	cloves garlic, minced	4
¼ cup	olive oil	½ cup
	Salt and black pepper	
¼ cup	panko bread crumbs	½ cup
¼ cup	grated Parmesan cheese	½ cup
2 Tbsp.	snipped fresh Italian parsley	¼ cup
⅛ tsp.	salt	¼ tsp.

Basil Halibut with Jalapeño Butter

A quick sauté of jalapeños in butter creates a richly flavored and slightly spicy drizzle for the fish. Serve it with slices of ripe tomato.

1. Brush fish with oil and sprinkle lightly with salt and pepper. Grill fish on a greased grill rack, covered, over medium heat for 4 to 6 minutes per ½-inch thickness or until fish flakes easily, turning once.

2. Meanwhile, heat butter in large skillet over medium heat. Add jalapenos; cook and stir 5 minutes or until tender and just beginning to lightly brown.

3. Spoon jalapeño-butter over fish and sprinkle with basil. Serve with lime wedges.

PER SERVING *419 cal., 31 g fat (13 g sat. fat), 148 mg chol., 370 mg sodium, 2 g carb., 1 g fiber, 33 g pro.*

START TO FINISH 20 minutes

4 servings	ingredients	8 servings
four 6-oz.	firm whitefish fillets (such as cod, halibut, or flounder), rinsed and patted dry	eight 6-oz.
1 Tbsp.	canola oil	2 Tbsp.
	Salt and black pepper	
6 Tbsp.	butter	¾ cup
2	jalapeño peppers, stemmed, seeded, and cut into thin strips (tip, page 12)	4
¼ cup	snipped fresh basil	½ cup
	Lime wedges	

Chipotle-Cilantro Tilapia

You'll never use up a whole can of chipotle peppers in adobo sauce in a single recipe, but they freeze well for future use. Divide the leftover chiles into several small bags and store in the freezer.

1. Thaw fish, if frozen. Rinse fish and pat dry with paper towels. Sprinkle with salt, cumin, chili powder, and black pepper.

2. In an extra-large nonstick skillet cook fish in hot oil over medium heat 6 to 8 minutes or until fish flakes easily, turning once.

3. Meanwhile, for yogurt sauce, in a bowl combine yogurt, cilantro, and chipotle peppers in adobo sauce. Serve fish with two warmed tortillas, yogurt sauce, and lime wedges.

PER SERVING *207 cal., 5 g fat (1 g sat. fat), 57 mg chol., 235 mg sodium, 15 g carb., 1 g fiber, 26 g pro.*

START TO FINISH 20 minutes

4 servings	ingredients	8 servings
four 4-oz.	fresh or frozen skinless tilapia fillets	eight 4-oz.
¼ tsp.	salt	½ tsp.
¼ tsp.	ground cumin	½ tsp.
⅛ tsp.	chipotle chili powder	¼ tsp.
⅛ tsp.	black pepper	¼ tsp.
2 tsp.	canola oil	4 tsp.
½ cup	plain nonfat yogurt	1 cup
2 Tbsp.	snipped fresh cilantro	¼ cup
½ to 1 tsp.	chipotle peppers in adobo sauce, minced (tip, page 12)	1 to 2 tsp.
eight 6-inch	corn tortillas, warmed	sixteen 6-inch
	Lime wedges	

Salmon Vera Cruz

Almost any kind of fish can be prepared "a la Veracruzana" (in the style of the coastal city of Vera Cruz on the Gulf of Mexico). It simply means with a fresh-tasting sauce featuring tomato, chiles, capers, and briny green olives.

1. Thaw salmon, if frozen. Preheat oven to 350°F. Rinse salmon; pat dry. If necessary, cut into six portions.

2. In a large skillet heat butter and oil over medium-high heat. Add orzo; cook and stir 5 minutes or until golden. Remove from heat; stir in broth. Return to heat. Simmer, uncovered, 8 minutes or just until orzo is tender and most of the liquid is absorbed. Stir in half the olives. Transfer to a 9×13-inch baking dish. Top with salmon.

3. Bake, covered, 20 to 25 minutes or until salmon flakes easily.

4. Meanwhile, in a bowl combine remaining olives and all remaining ingredients. Spoon over salmon and orzo.

FOR 12 SERVINGS Cut salmon into 12 portions and use two 9×13-inch baking pans.

PER SERVING *386 cal., 13 g fat (3 g sat. fat), 67 mg chol., 465 mg sodium, 37 g carb., 2 g fiber, 29 g pro.*

PREP 30 minutes
BAKE 20 minutes at 350°F

6 servings	ingredients	12 servings
1½ lb.	fresh or frozen skinless salmon fillet, about ¾ inch thick	3 lb.
1 Tbsp.	butter	2 Tbsp.
1 Tbsp.	olive oil	2 Tbsp.
1½ cups	dried orzo pasta	3 cups
3 cups	vegetable broth or reduced-sodium chicken broth	6 cups
¼ cup	pimiento-stuffed green olives, sliced	½ cup
2 cups	chopped tomatoes	4 cups
1	jalapeño pepper, seeded and finely chopped (tip, page 12)	2
2 Tbsp.	lime juice	¼ cup
1 Tbsp.	capers, drained	2 Tbsp.
½ tsp.	sugar	1 tsp.

Lemon-Herb Roasted Salmon with Broccoli and Tomatoes

When you need a quick and healthful fish dish, look no further than this all-in-one-pan recipe.

1. Thaw salmon, if frozen. Preheat oven to 400°F. Line a 15×10-inch baking pan with parchment paper if desired. Rinse salmon; pat dry. Cut salmon into portions and place on prepared pan. Drizzle with half the oil. Sprinkle with half the oregano, the salt, and pepper.

2. In a bowl combine tomatoes, broccoli, garlic, and remaining oil and oregano. Sprinkle lightly with additional salt and pepper; toss to coat. Place in pan with salmon. Roast 15 to 18 minutes or just until salmon flakes easily.

3. Meanwhile, remove 1 tsp. zest and squeeze 3 Tbsp. juice from lemon. In a small bowl combine lemon zest and juice and remaining ingredients. Spoon over salmon and vegetables.

FOR 8 SERVINGS Use two 15×10-inch baking pans. In Step 3, remove 2 tsp. zest and 6 Tbsp. juice from lemon.

PER SERVING *276 cal., 14 g fat (2 g sat. fat), 62 mg chol., 362 mg sodium, 13 g carb., 3 g fiber, 25 g pro.*

PREP 20 minutes
ROAST 15 minutes at 400°F

4 servings	ingredients	8 servings
one 1-lb.	fresh or frozen skinless salmon fillet	two 1-lb.
2 Tbsp.	olive oil	¼ cup
1½ tsp.	dried oregano, crushed	1 Tbsp.
¼ tsp.	salt	½ tsp.
⅛ tsp.	black pepper	¼ tsp.
2 cups	grape or cherry tomatoes, halved	4 cups
2 cups	broccoli florets	4 cups
2	cloves garlic, minced	4
1	lemon	2
2 Tbsp.	snipped fresh basil	¼ cup
1 Tbsp.	snipped fresh Italian parsley	2 Tbsp.
1 Tbsp.	honey	2 Tbsp.

Salmon with Tomatoes and Olives

The acidity of the tomatoes and brininess of the olives in this dish are a nice complement to the rich flavor and texture of the salmon.

4 servings	ingredients	8 servings
four 4-oz.	fresh or frozen skinless salmon fillets	eight 4-oz.
	Salt and black pepper	
1 Tbsp.	olive oil	2 Tbsp.
¼ cup	sliced shallots	½ cup
2	cloves garlic, minced	4
2 cups	red and/or yellow grape or cherry tomatoes, halved if large	4 cups
½ cup	halved pitted Kalamata olives	1 cup
	Zest of 1 small orange, cut into strips	
	Small fresh oregano leaves	
	Orange wedges	

1. Thaw salmon, if frozen. Rinse salmon; pat dry with paper towels; season with salt and pepper. in an extra-large nonstick skillet cook salmon in hot oil over medium-high heat 6 to 8 minutes or just until fish flakes easily, turning once. Remove fish from skillet; cover to keep warm.

2. In the same skillet cook shallots and garlic over medium heat 2 to 3 minutes or until tender. Add tomatoes; cook 2 to 3 minutes or until tomatoes soften and begin to juice. Stir in olives and orange zest.

3. Return salmon to skillet. Sprinkle with fresh oregano and serve with orange wedges.

PER SERVING *257 cal., 13 g fat (2 g sat. fat), 62 mg chol., 316 mg sodium, 11 g carb., 3 g fiber, 24 g pro.*

Salmon with Roasted Tomatoes and Shallots

Just a handful of ingredients and very little prep time create a very flavorful dish thanks to lots of garlic and shallots and fresh oregano.

1. Thaw salmon, if frozen. Rinse salmon and pat dry. Lightly sprinkle with salt and pepper. Preheat oven to 400°F.

2. Lightly coat a 9×13-inch baking dish with cooking spray. Combine the remaining ingredients in prepared dish; toss to coat.

3. Roast tomato mixture, uncovered, 15 minutes. Place salmon, skin side down, on roasted tomatoes. Continue to roast, uncovered, 15 to 18 minutes or until salmon flakes easily.

FOR 8 SERVINGS Use two 9×13-inch baking dishes.

*TIP As a substitute, for 4 servings, use 1½ tsp. dried oregano, crushed, for the fresh. For 8 servings, use 1 Tbsp. dried oregano, crushed, for the fresh.

PER SERVING *320 cal., 19 g fat (4 g sat. fat), 62 mg chol., 297 mg sodium, 12 g carb., 2 g fiber, 26 g pro.*

PREP 20 minutes
ROAST 30 minutes at 400°F

4 servings	ingredients	8 servings
one 1-lb.	fresh or frozen salmon fillet, skinned if desired	two 1-lb.
	Salt and black pepper	
	Nonstick cooking spray	
4 cups	grape tomatoes	8 cups
½ cup	thinly sliced shallots	1 cup
6	cloves garlic, minced	12
2 Tbsp.	snipped fresh oregano*	¼ cup
1 Tbsp.	olive oil	2 Tbsp.
¼ tsp.	salt	½ tsp.
¼ tsp.	black pepper	½ tsp.

Salmon Patties with Parsley Mayo

Starting with pouches of cooked salmon—which is much higher in quality than canned salmon—makes these salmon patties go together in a snap.

1. In a medium bowl combine salmon, bread crumbs, sweet pepper, green onions, egg, 2 Tbsp. of the mayonnaise, and the mustard. Shape into eight 2½-inch patties (about ⅓ cup each).

2. Coat an extra-large nonstick skillet with cooking spray and heat over medium heat. Add patties and cook 4 to 5 minutes or until browned. Lightly coat patty tops with cooking spray; turn. Cook 4 to 5 minutes more or until browned and cooked through (160°F.).

3. For parsley mayo, in a bowl stir together the remaining mayonnaise, parsley, lemon juice, and hot sauce.

FOR 8 SERVINGS In Step 1, use ¼ cup of the mayonnaise. In Step 2, cook patties in batches, if necessary.

PER SERVING *422 cal., 33 g fat (7 g sat. fat), 99 mg chol., 852 mg sodium, 8 g carb., 1 g fiber, 22 g pro.*

START TO FINISH 25 minutes

4 servings	ingredients	8 servings
three 5-oz. pouches	skinless, boneless pink salmon	six 5-oz. pouches
½ cup	panko bread crumbs	1 cup
½ cup	finely chopped red sweet pepper	1 cup
½ cup	finely chopped green onions	1 cup
1	egg, lightly beaten	2
½ cup	mayonnaise	1 cup
1 Tbsp.	yellow mustard	2 Tbsp.
	Nonstick cooking spray	
3 Tbsp.	finely chopped fresh Italian parsley	⅓ cup
1 Tbsp.	lemon juice or white vinegar	2 Tbsp.
1 tsp.	bottled hot pepper sauce	2 tsp.

Creamy Tuna-Noodle Toss

In the hierarchy of comfort food, tuna-noodle casserole is right near the top. This saucepan version is quick comfort—it takes just 30 minutes start to finish—and uses ingredients you might very well have in your pantry, freezer, and refrigerator.

1. Cook noodles according to package directions, adding peas the last 2 minutes of cooking. Drain and return to pan.

2. Meanwhile, in a medium saucepan melt butter. Add onion, garlic, and pepper; cook and stir over medium heat 3 minutes or just until onion is tender. Stir in flour until blended. Add milk all at once. Cook and stir until thickened and bubbly. Remove from heat; add tuna and half the cheese.

3. Pour tuna mixture over noodles and peas in pan. Toss gently to combine. If desired, stir in additional milk, 1 Tbsp. at time, until desired consistency. Season to taste with salt and pepper. Drizzle with lemon juice. Sprinkle with remaining cheese and additional pepper.

PER SERVING *438 cal., 16 g fat (9 g sat. fat), 89 mg chol., 614 mg sodium, 48 g carb., 4 g fiber, 25 g pro.*

START TO FINISH 30 minutes

4 servings	ingredients	8 servings
6 oz.	wide egg noodles	12 oz.
1½ cups	frozen peas	3 cups
3 Tbsp.	butter	6 Tbsp.
1	small red onion, quartered and sliced	2
2	cloves garlic, minced	4
¼ tsp.	freshly ground black pepper	½ tsp.
2 Tbsp.	all-purpose flour	¼ cup
1¼ cups	milk	2½ cups
one 5-oz. can	solid white tuna, drained and broken into chunks	two 5-oz. cans
½ cup	grated Parmesan cheese	1 cup
	Milk	
	Salt and freshly ground black pepper	
1 Tbsp.	fresh lemon juice	2 Tbsp.

Lemony Tuna Salad

For a salad like this, you want the highest-quality canned tuna you can find. For the best flavor and texture, look for solid white albacore or chunk white tuna packed in oil.

1. Remove 1 tsp. zest and squeeze 3 Tbsp. juice from lemon.

2. In a large bowl combine lemon zest and juice, fennel, and onion. Add arugula, tuna, and tomatoes; toss gently to coat. Season to taste with salt and pepper.

FOR 8 SERVINGS Remove 2 tsp. zest and squeeze 6 Tbsp. juice from lemon.

PER SERVING *104 cal., 2 g fat (1 g sat. fat), 24 mg chol., 377 mg sodium, 7 g carb., 2 g fiber, 15 g pro.*

START TO FINISH 20 minutes

4 servings	ingredients	8 servings
1	lemon	2
½ cup	chopped fennel	1 cup
½ cup	thinly sliced red onion	1 cup
one 5-oz. pkg.	arugula or mixed spring green	two 5-oz. pkg.
two 5-oz. cans	tuna, drained	four 5-oz. cans
1 cup	grape or cherry tomatoes, halved	2 cups
	Sea salt and black pepper	

Tuna-Noodle Casserole

Switch up the protein in this classic casserole to make it with tuna, salmon, chicken, or ham.

1. Preheat oven to 375°F. Lightly grease an 11×7-inch baking dish. In a large pot cook noodles according to package directions. Drain; return noodles to pot.

2. Meanwhile, for sauce, in a large saucepan melt butter over medium heat. Add sweet pepper, celery, and onion; cook 8 to 10 minutes or until tender, stirring occasionally. Stir in flour, mustard, salt, and black pepper. Add milk all at once; cook and stir until slightly thickened and bubbly.

3. Gently fold sauce and tuna into cooked noodles. Transfer to the prepared baking dish. In a bowl stir together the remaining ingredients. Sprinkle crumb mixture over noodle mixture.

4. Bake, uncovered, 25 to 30 minutes or until heated. Let stand 5 minutes before serving.

FOR 8 SERVINGS Use a 9×13-inch baking dish.

*TIP To substitute for the tuna, for 4 servings use two 6-oz. cans skinless, boneless salmon, drained; 1 cup shredded cooked chicken breast; or 1 cup julienned low-sodium ham. For 8 servings use four 6-oz. cans salmon, 2 cups shredded chicken breast, or 2 cups julienned ham.

PER SERVING *486 cal., 20 g fat (11 g sat. fat), 113 mg chol., 779 mg sodium, 47 g carb., 3 g fiber, 28 g pro.*

PREP 30 minutes
BAKE 25 minutes at 375°F
STAND 5 minutes

4 servings	ingredients	8 servings
3 cups	dried wide noodles	6 cups
¼ cup	butter, cut up	½ cup
1 cup	chopped red sweet pepper	2 cups
½ cup	chopped celery	1 cup
¼ cup	chopped onion	½ cup
¼ cup	all-purpose flour	½ cup
1 Tbsp.	Dijon mustard	2 Tbsp.
¼ tsp.	salt	½ tsp.
¼ tsp.	black pepper	½ tsp.
2¼ cups	fat-free milk	4½ cups
one 12-oz. can	chunk white tuna (water pack), drained and broken into chunks*	two 12-oz. cans
½ cup	panko bread crumbs	1 cup
¼ cup	grated Parmesan cheese	½ cup
1 Tbsp.	snipped fresh Italian parsley	2 Tbsp.
1 Tbsp.	butter, melted	2 Tbsp.

Grilled Shrimp in Coconut Milk Sauce

Serve this sweet and spicy Indonesian-style dish with hot cooked rice or roasted sweet potato wedges.

1. Thaw shrimp, if frozen. Peel and devein shrimp, leaving tails intact if desired. Rinse shrimp; pat dry. In a bowl combine half the oil, the lime juice, half the chile pepper and garlic, and the salt and black pepper. Add shrimp; toss to coat. Cover and marinate in the refrigerator 30 to 60 minutes, stirring occasionally.

2. Meanwhile, if using wooden skewers, soak in water 30 minutes. For sauce, in a medium skillet heat remaining oil over medium heat. Add sweet pepper, onion, and remaining chile pepper and garlic; cook 10 minutes or until tender, stirring occasionally. Add tomatoes, coconut milk, and tomato paste. Bring to boiling; reduce heat. Simmer, uncovered, 5 minutes or until desired consistency. Season to taste with additional salt. Keep warm.

3. Thread shrimp onto four long skewers, leaving ¼ inch between pieces. Grill shrimp on a greased rack, uncovered, over medium heat for 7 to 9 minutes or until shrimp are opaque, turning once.

4. Serve shrimp kabobs with sauce and sprinkle with parsley.

FOR 8 SERVINGS Use 8 long skewers.

*TIP Stir coconut milk before measuring.

PER SERVING *195 cal., 10 g fat (6 g sat. fat), 129 mg chol., 327 mg sodium, 6 g carb., 1 g fiber, 19 g pro.*

PREP 35 minutes
MARINATE 30 minutes
GRILL 7 minutes

4 servings	ingredients	8 servings
1 lb.	fresh or frozen extra-large shrimp in shells	2 lb.
2 Tbsp.	olive oil	¼ cup
2 tsp.	lime juice	4 tsp.
1	fresh bird chile pepper or chile de arbol, finely chopped (tip, page 12)	2
2	cloves garlic, minced	4
⅛ tsp.	salt	¼ tsp.
⅛ tsp.	black pepper	¼ tsp.
½ cup	chopped red sweet pepper	1 cup
¼ cup	finely chopped onion	½ cup
1 cup	peeled, seeded, and chopped tomatoes	2 cups
½ cup	unsweetened coconut milk*	1 cup
1 Tbsp.	tomato paste	2 Tbsp.
	Snipped fresh parsley or cilantro	

Baked Shrimp and Rice

This creamy dish studded with tender shrimp is surprisingly easy but elegant enough for company. Serve it with steamed and buttered green beans.

1. Thaw shrimp, if frozen. Preheat oven to 350°F. In a large saucepan heat butter over medium heat until melted. Add onion and sweet pepper; cook until tender, stirring occasionally. Remove from heat.

2. Stir shrimp, cooked rice, soup, half-and-half, sherry, lemon juice, salt, and cayenne pepper into vegetables. Transfer to an 8×8-inch baking dish.

3. Bake, uncovered, 30 minutes or until heated through. Sprinkle with almonds and cilantro.

FOR 12 SERVINGS Use a 9×13-inch baking dish.

PER SERVING *290 cal., 13 g fat (5 g sat. fat), 141 mg chol., 624 mg sodium, 23 g carb., 1 g fiber, 19 g pro.*

PREP 30 minutes
BAKE 30 minutes at 350°F

6 servings	ingredients	12 servings
12 oz.	fresh or frozen peeled, deveined cooked shrimp	24 oz.
2 Tbsp.	butter	¼ cup
½ cup	chopped onion	1 cup
¼ cup	chopped green or red sweet pepper	½ cup
2 cups	cooked white rice	4 cups
one 10.75-oz. can	condensed cream of shrimp or cream of celery soup	two 10.75-oz. cans
½ cup	half-and-half or light cream	1 cup
2 Tbsp.	dry sherry	¼ cup
1 tsp.	lemon juice	2 tsp.
¼ tsp.	salt	½ tsp.
⅛ tsp.	cayenne pepper	¼ tsp.
3 Tbsp.	sliced almonds, toasted (tip, page 19)	6 Tbsp.
	Snipped fresh cilantro	

Spicy Shrimp with Cabbage-Noodle Slaw

Packed with veggies, this crunchy noodle dish hits the spot on a warm summer night.

1. Thaw shrimp, if frozen. Rinse shrimp; pat dry with paper towels. In a large skillet heat oil over medium heat. Add garlic and crushed red pepper; cook and stir 30 seconds. Add shrimp; cook and stir 3 to 4 minutes or until shrimp are opaque. Remove from heat.

2. In a large saucepan cook noodles in lightly salted boiling water 2 to 3 minutes or just until tender; drain. Snip noodles into shorter lengths.

3. In an extra-large bowl combine noodles and the next seven ingredients (through cilantro). Pour Lime-Ginger Dressing over slaw; toss gently to coat. Top slaw with shrimp and sprinkle with almonds.

LIME-GINGER DRESSING In a bowl whisk together 3 Tbsp. vegetable oil, 2 Tbsp. lime juice, 2 Tbsp. rice vinegar, 2 tsp. grated fresh ginger, 2 tsp. honey, 2 tsp. soy sauce, ½ tsp. salt, and ¼ tsp. cayenne pepper.

FOR 16 SERVINGS For the Lime-Ginger Dressing, use ⅓ cup oil, ¼ cup lime juice, ¼ cup rice vinegar, 4 tsp. grated fresh ginger, 4 tsp. honey, 4 tsp. soy sauce, 1 tsp. salt, and ½ tsp. cayenne pepper.

PER SERVING *249 cal., 10 g fat (1 g sat. fat), 129 mg chol., 405 mg sodium, 20 g carb., 2 g fiber, 20 g pro.*

START TO FINISH 40 minutes

8 servings	ingredients	16 servings
1½ lb.	fresh or frozen peeled, deveined large shrimp	3 lb.
1 Tbsp.	vegetable oil	2 Tbsp.
4	cloves garlic, minced	8
1 tsp.	crushed red pepper	2 tsp.
4 oz.	dried rice vermicelli	8 oz.
4 cups	shredded napa cabbage	8 cups
1 cup	shredded bok choy	2 cups
1 cup	coarsely shredded carrots	2 cups
½ cup	thinly sliced radishes	1 cup
½ cup	strips cucumber	1 cup
½ cup	strips red sweet pepper	1 cup
¼ cup	snipped fresh cilantro	½ cup
	Lime-Ginger Dressing	
¼ cup	sliced almonds, toasted (tip, page 19)	½ cup

Basil Shrimp Chowder

Mascarpone cheese—an Italian cream cheese— gives this chowder its rich, creamy texture. If you can't find it, you can substitute 4 ounces of cream cheese whipped with 2 tablespoons of heavy cream for 4 servings or 8 ounces of cream cheese whipped with ¼ cup heavy cream for 8 servings.

1. Melt butter in a large pot over medium heat. Add celery, onion, and sweet pepper. Cook and stir 5 minutes or until tender. Stir in flour until coated. Add water, clam juice, seasoning, and basil. Bring to boiling; reduce heat.

2. Stir in shrimp, corn, and capers. Cook 2 to 5 minutes or until shrimp are bright pink. Remove from heat. Stir in cheese until melted. Top with fresh basil if desired.

PER SERVING *267 cal., 16 g fat (9 g sat. fat), 167 mg chol., 449 mg sodium, 13 g carb., 2 g fiber, 18 g pro.*

PREP 20 minutes
COOK 20 minutes

4 servings	ingredients	8 servings
1 Tbsp.	butter	2 Tbsp.
½ cup	finely chopped celery	1 cup
½ cup	chopped red onion	1 cup
¼ cup	finely chopped green sweet pepper	½ cup
1 Tbsp.	all-purpose flour	2 Tbsp.
1 cup	water	2 cups
one 8-oz. bottle	clam juice	two 8-oz. bottles
1 tsp.	Old Bay seasoning	2 tsp.
½ tsp.	dried basil, crushed	1 tsp.
¾ lb.	large shrimp, peeled with tails on	1½ lb.
half 12-oz. pkg.	frozen whole kernel corn	one 12-oz. pkg.
1 Tbsp.	capers	2 Tbsp.
half 8-oz. container	mascarpone cheese	one 8-oz. container
	Fresh basil leaves (optional)	

Thai Coconut and Basmati Rice with Seared Scallops

The key to getting a good sear on scallops so they get that beautiful (and tasty!) brown crust is to make sure they are very dry when they go into the hot pan.

PREP 20 minutes
COOK 20 minutes

4 servings	ingredients	8 servings
1 lb.	fresh or frozen sea scallops	2 lb.
½ tsp.	salt	1 tsp.
½ cup	chopped onion	1 cup
2 tsp.	olive oil	4 tsp.
½ cup	uncooked basmati rice	1 cup
¾ cup	unsweetened light coconut milk	1½ cups
¼ cup	reduced-sodium chicken broth	½ cup
¼ cup	water	½ cup
¼ tsp.	black pepper	½ tsp.
1	medium mango, seeded, peeled, and coarsely chopped	2
¼ cup	snipped fresh basil	½ cup
1 Tbsp.	olive oil	2 Tbsp.
	Fresh basil leaves (optional)	

1. Thaw scallops, if frozen. Rinse scallops; pat dry with paper towels. Sprinkle scallops with half the salt.

2. In a medium saucepan cook onion in 2 tsp. hot oil over medium heat 5 to 7 minutes or until tender. Stir in rice. Cook and stir 1 minute. Stir in coconut milk, broth, the water, remaining salt, and the pepper. Bring to boiling; reduce heat. Simmer, covered, 20 minutes or until rice is tender and liquid is absorbed. Stir in mango and the snipped basil.

3. Meanwhile, in a large nonstick skillet cook scallops in the 1 Tbsp. hot oil over medium-high heat 2 to 3 minutes or until opaque and golden brown, turning once. Serve scallops over rice. If desired, sprinkle with basil leaves.

FOR 8 SERVINGS In Step 2, cook onion in 4 tsp. hot oil. In Step 3, cook scallops in 2 Tbsp. hot oil.

PER SERVING *299 cal., 9 g fat (3 g sat. fat), 37 mg chol., 518 mg sodium, 32 g carb., 1 g fiber, 22 g pro.*

CHAPTER 5

Sides

These savory salads, veggies, grains, soups, and breads turn even the simplest main dish into a special meal— and there are options for every taste and occasion.

135 Summer Spaghetti Salad

136 Penne and Asparagus Salad

137 Peanutty Noodle Slaw

138 Shaved Brussels Sprouts with Green Onion Vinaigrette

140 Roasted Radishes with Orange Vinaigrette

141 Roasted Cabbage with Pears

145 Spice-and-Honey Roasted Carrots

146 French-Style Green Beans with Lemon and Walnuts

147 Zesty Green Bean Slaw

148 Harvest Succotash

149 Farmer's Salad

150 Confetti Corn Salad

151 Tex-Mex Potato Salad

151 Zucchini and Crispy Potato Salad

152 Easy Hash Brown Bake

155 Basil and Olive Potatoes

156 Mexican Red Rice

157 Pear and Sweet Potato Soup

159 Savory Double-Walnut Scones

141

150

157

Summer Spaghetti Salad

"Noodles" made of spiralized zucchini and summer squash add color and crunch to this surprising pasta salad.

1. Heat 2 Tbsp. of the oil in an extra-large skillet over medium heat. Add garlic and stir 1 minute. Add pasta, toss to combine. Add broth; cook, uncovered, over medium heat 10 minutes or until liquid is nearly absorbed, stirring occasionally. Remove from heat; cool 10 minutes. Transfer to a serving dish. Meanwhile, use a spiral vegetable slicer to cut zucchini and yellow squash into long strands. Snip strands into shorter lengths if desired. Add to spaghetti. Cool completely. Pull cheese into thin strands; chill until ready to serve.

2. In a bowl toss together tomatoes, onion, parsley, salt, pepper, remaining oil, and vinegar. Add string cheese to spaghetti mixture. Top with tomato mixture and walnuts.

FOR 20 SERVINGS In Step 1, use ¼ cup oil.

*TIP To toast walnuts for 10-serving salad, combine walnuts, 1 tsp. olive oil, and ¼ tsp. kosher salt in a baking pan. Bake in a 350°F oven 5 minutes or until toasted. For 20 servings, use 2 tsp. olive oil and ½ tsp. kosher salt.

PER SERVING *335 cal., 19 g fat (4 g sat. fat), 9 mg chol., 443 mg sodium, 33 g carb., 2 g fiber, 12 g pro.*

PREP 30 minutes
COOK 10 minutes
COOL 10 minutes

10 servings	ingredients	20 servings
½ cup	olive oil	1 cup
3	cloves garlic, sliced	6
one 12-oz. pkg.	spaghetti, broken in half	two 12-oz. pkg.
3 cups	reduced-sodium chicken broth	6 cups
1	medium zucchini, ends trimmed	2
1	medium yellow summer squash, ends trimmed	2
6	sticks string cheese	12
4 cups	red and yellow cherry tomatoes, halved	8 cups
1 cup	finely chopped onion	2 cups
1 cup	chopped fresh Italian parsley	2 cups
1 tsp.	kosher salt	2 tsp.
½ tsp.	freshly ground black pepper	1 tsp.
¼ cup	red wine vinegar	½ tsp.
½ cup	walnuts, toasted*	1 cup

Penne and Asparagus Salad

Don't overcook the asparagus—and be sure to rinse it immediately in cold water after cooking to keep it fresh, crisp and bright green.

1. In a large Dutch oven cook pasta according to package directions, adding asparagus the last 2 minutes of cooking; drain. Rinse with cold water; drain again. Transfer to a large bowl.

2. Stir in the next six ingredients (through Gouda cheese). Add dressing; stir to coat. Cover and chill 2 to 24 hours. Stir in basil before serving.

PER SERVING *263 cal., 15 g fat (5 g sat. fat), 22 mg chol., 581 mg sodium, 20 g carb., 1 g fiber, 10 g pro.*

PREP 30 minutes
CHILL 2 hours

10 servings	ingredients	20 servings
8 oz.	dried penne pasta	16 oz.
8 oz.	asparagus spears, trimmed and cut into 1½-inch pieces	16 oz.
½ cup	chopped red sweet pepper	1 cup
½ cup	halved, pitted Kalamata olives	1 cup
3 oz.	capocollo or prosciutto, thinly sliced and coarsely chopped	6 oz.
3 oz.	Fontina cheese, cut into ¼-inch cubes	6 oz.
2 oz.	sharp cheddar cheese, cut into ¼-inch cubes	4 oz.
2 oz.	Gouda cheese, cut into ¼-inch cubes	4 oz.
¾ cup	creamy garlic or creamy Italian salad dressing	1½ cups
¼ cup	coarsely snipped fresh basil	½ cup

Peanutty Noodle Slaw

There seems to be some version of ramen salad at nearly every potluck. This take is light on the ramen, heavy on crunchy veggies, and has the added enticement of a flavorful creamy ginger-sesame-peanut dressing.

1. For dressing, in a screw-top jar combine Asian dressing and peanut butter. Cover and shake well, adding 1 to 2 Tbsp. water if necessary to reach desired consistency.

2. In a large bowl combine cabbage, green onions, and sesame seeds. Break ramen noodles into small pieces and add to cabbage mixture. Drizzle with dressing; toss gently to coat. Cover and chill 30 minutes to 2 hours. Sprinkle with peanuts.

FOR 16 SERVINGS In Step 1, use 2 to 4 Tbsp. water to thin dressing.

PER SERVING *218 cal., 14 g fat (3 g sat. fat), 0 mg chol., 345 mg sodium, 18 g carb., 3 g fiber, 6 g pro.*

PREP 25 minutes
CHILL 30 minutes

8 servings	ingredients	16 servings
¾ cup	bottled Asian ginger sesame salad dressing	1½ cups
2 Tbsp.	creamy peanut butter	¼ cup
6 cups	shredded coleslaw mix or shredded broccoli slaw mix	12 cups
⅓ cup	thinly sliced green onions	⅔ cup
2 Tbsp.	sesame seeds, toasted (tip, page 19)	4 Tbsp.
one 3-oz. pkg.	chicken-flavor ramen noodles (save seasoning packet for another use)	two 3-oz. pkg.
½ cup	chopped peanuts	1 cup

Shaved Brussels Sprouts with Green Onion Vinaigrette

Slicing or shaving your own Brussels sprouts gives you the best, freshest results, but if you're in a hurry, you can use packaged presliced sprouts.

8 servings	ingredients	16 servings
4	green onions	8
¼ cup	olive oil	½ cup
¼ cup	lemon juice	½ cup
1 Tbsp.	white wine vinegar	2 Tbsp.
1 Tbsp.	honey	2 Tbsp.
1 tsp.	ground coriander	2 tsp.
½ tsp.	kosher salt	1 tsp.
1 lb.	Brussels sprouts, trimmed and very thinly sliced*	2 lb.
2	oranges, peeled and sectioned	4
1 cup	cashews, toasted (tip, page 19)	2 cups

1. For dressing, chop green onions, separating white parts from green tops. In a blender or food processor combine white parts of onions and the next six ingredients (through salt). Cover and blend or process until smooth.

2. In a large bowl combine Brussels sprouts and green tops of onions. Pour dressing over sprouts; toss gently to coat. Stir in oranges and cashews.

TO MAKE AHEAD Prepare as directed. Cover and chill up to 4 hours.

*TIP To trim Brussels sprouts, cut off the stems where leaves start to grow. Remove dark green outer leaves until tender light green leaves are uniformly exposed. You can also use a food processor to shave Brussels sprouts or purchase them already shaved.

PER SERVING *162 cal., 11 g fat (2 g sat. fat), 0 mg chol., 140 mg sodium, 15 g carb., 3 g fiber, 4 g pro.*

Roasted Radishes with Orange Vinaigrette

Roasting radishes sweetens them and softens some of their bite. They make an interesting side dish to roast chicken or a grilled steak.

PREP 15 minutes
ROAST 30 minutes at 425°F

6 servings	ingredients	12 servings
1½ lb.	radishes, trimmed and halved	3 lb.
3 Tbsp.	olive oil	6 Tbsp.
1	orange	1
1 Tbsp.	sherry vinegar or white wine vinegar	2 Tbsp.
1 tsp.	honey	2 tsp.
	Salt and black pepper	

1. Preheat oven to 425°F. Place radishes in a 15×10-inch baking pan. Drizzle with 1 Tbsp. of the oil; toss to coat. Roast 30 to 35 minutes or until tender and lightly browned, stirring once.

2. Meanwhile, remove ½ tsp. zest and squeeze 1 Tbsp. juice from orange. For vinaigrette, in a small screw-top jar combine orange zest and juice, vinegar, honey, and remaining oil. Cover and shake well. Season to taste with salt and pepper. Drizzle vinaigrette over radishes.

FOR 12 SERVINGS In Step 1, use 2 Tbsp. of the oil and two 15×10-inch baking pans. In Step 2, use 1 tsp. zest and 2 Tbsp. juice from orange

PER SERVING *83 cal., 7 g fat (1 g sat. fat), 0 mg chol., 141 mg sodium, 5 g carb., 2 g fiber, 1 g pro.*

Roasted Cabbage with Pears

Two fall favorites—one vegetable and one fruit—come together in this simple side dish. Toasted walnuts add crunch and blue cheese a bit of tanginess. It's perfect as an accompaniment to pork chops or pork roast.

1. Preheat oven to 425°F. Place cabbage wedges in a 15×10-inch baking pan. Drizzle with oil and sprinkle with salt and pepper.

2. Roast 35 to 40 minutes or until tender, turning cabbage once and adding pears the last 10 to 15 minutes.

3. Drizzle lemon juice over cabbage and pears. Sprinkle with walnuts and cheese.

FOR 8 SERVINGS Use two 15×10-inch baking pans.

PER SERVING *364 cal., 25 g fat (5 g sat. fat), 11 mg chol., 529 mg sodium, 32 g carb., 10 g fiber, 10 g pro.*

PREP 15 minutes
ROAST 35 minutes at 425°F

4 servings	ingredients	8 servings
one 1½-lb. head	savoy, green, or red cabbage, trimmed and cut into 8 wedges	two 1½-lb. heads
	Olive oil	
	Salt and black pepper	
3	pears, halved lengthwise	6
2 Tbsp.	fresh lemon juice	¼ cup
¾ cup	chopped walnuts, toasted (tip, page 19)	1½ cups
½ cup	crumbled blue cheese	1 cup

Spice-and-Honey Roasted Carrots

A little bit of honey sweetens the deal in this dish seasoned with a trio of Middle Eastern spices—coriander, sesame, and cumin. Toasting and grinding the seeds results in the freshest, most intense flavor.

1. Preheat oven to 425°F. Trim and peel carrots if desired. Cut large carrots lengthwise.

2. Line a 15×10-inch baking pan with foil or parchment. Spread carrots in prepared pan. Drizzle with olive oil. Roast, uncovered, 20 minutes.

3. Meanwhile, heat a skillet over medium-high heat. Add hazelnuts; cook 3 minutes or until fragrant and toasted, stirring occasionally. Transfer nuts to a bowl. Add seeds to hot skillet. Cook over medium-high heat 2 minutes or until fragrant and toasted, stirring constantly. Remove spices from heat and transfer to another bowl; cool 10 minutes.

4. Using a spice or coffee grinder or mortar and pestle, grind or crush toasted spices just until coarsely ground. Add the hazelnuts, salt, and pepper, crushing nuts slightly. Remove carrots from oven. Drizzle with honey; toss to coat. Sprinkle carrots with half the hazelnut mixture. Roast 5 to 10 minutes or until carrots are tender.

5. Transfer carrots to a serving platter. Sprinkle with more nut seasoning and, if desired, drizzle with additional honey.

FOR 12 SERVINGS Use two 15×10-inch baking pans.

PER SERVING *152 cal., 9 g fat (1 g sat. fat), 0 mg chol., 274 mg sodium, 17 g carb., 5 g fiber, 3 g pro.*

PREP 20 minutes
ROAST 25 minutes at 425°F

6 servings	ingredients	12 servings
1½ lb.	regular or tricolor carrots	3 lb.
1 Tbsp.	olive oil	2 Tbsp.
½ cup	coarsely chopped hazelnuts (filberts)	1 cup
1 Tbsp.	coriander seeds	2 Tbsp.
1 Tbsp.	sesame seeds	2 Tbsp.
1½ tsp.	cumin seeds	1 Tbsp.
½ tsp.	salt	1 tsp.
¼ tsp.	black pepper	½ tsp.
1 Tbsp.	honey	2 Tbsp.

French-Style Green Beans with Lemon and Walnuts

This simple side makes a light, beautiful, bright green addition to a holiday table laden with otherwise rich dishes.

1. In a medium saucepan cook beans, covered, in a small amount of boiling salted water 5 to 10 minutes or until crisp-tender; drain.

2. Meanwhile, remove ¼ tsp. zest and 1 tsp. juice from lemon. In a small saucepan melt butter over medium heat. Add walnuts and ginger; cook 2 to 3 minutes or until nuts are toasted. Remove from heat; stir in lemon zest and juice. Stir into cooked beans.

FOR 8 SERVINGS Remove ½ tsp. zest and 2 tsp. juice from lemon.

PER SERVING *100 cal., 8 g fat (2 g sat. fat), 8 mg chol., 35 mg sodium, 7 g carb., 3 g fiber, 3 g pro.*

PREP 20 minutes
COOK 5 minutes

4 servings	ingredients	8 servings
12 oz.	fresh green beans, trimmed and sliced lengthwise	24 oz.
1	lemon	1
1 Tbsp.	butter	2 Tbsp.
¼ cup	chopped walnuts	½ cup
1 tsp.	grated fresh ginger	2 tsp.

Zesty Green Bean Slaw

Fresno peppers are similar to jalapeños in hotness, but they can be green or red. Similarly, Thai chiles can be green or red. They are much smaller—and hotter—than Fresno peppers.

1. In a large pot of lightly salted water cook green beans 2 minutes. Drain; immediately transfer to a large bowl of ice water to stop the cooking.

2. For the dressing, in a screw-top jar combine lime juice, fish sauce, sugar, and garlic. Cover and shake well.

3. Drain green beans; place in a large bowl. Add cabbage and cilantro. Add dressing; toss gently to coat. Cover and chill up to 1 hour. Sprinkle with peanuts and chile pepper.

PER SERVING *126 cal., 7 g fat (1 g sat. fat), 0 mg chol., 629 mg sodium, 13 g carb., 3 g fiber, 5 g pro.*

PREP 20 minutes
CHILL 1 hour

10 servings	ingredients	20 servings
1 lb.	thin green beans, trimmed and cut up	2 lb.
6 Tbsp.	lime juice	¾ cup
¼ cup	fish sauce	½ cup
¼ cup	sugar	½ cup
2	cloves garlic, minced	4
8 cups	shredded napa cabbage	16 cups
1 cup	cilantro leaves and stems, chopped	2 cups
1 cup	coarsely chopped salted peanuts	2 cups
1	fresh Fresno or Thai chile pepper, thinly sliced (tip, page 12)	2

Harvest Succotash

Mustard greens add peppery flavor—and terrific nutrition—to this brightly colored succotash.

1. In an extra-large skillet cook bacon over medium heat until crisp. With a slotted spoon remove bacon from skillet and drain on paper towels. Add garlic to skillet; cook 30 seconds. Stir in the mustard greens, corn, and beans; cook and stir 3 minutes or until mustard greens soften. Stir in half-and-half, sage, salt, and pepper. Bring to boiling. Transfer to a serving dish. Sprinkle with reserved bacon.

PER SERVING *170 cal., 7 g fat (3 g sat. fat), 15 mg chol., 262 mg sodium, 21 g carb., 4 g fiber, 7 g pro.*

START TO FINISH 25 minutes

8 servings	ingredients	16 servings
2	slices bacon, chopped	4
1	clove garlic, sliced	2
4 cups	finely chopped mustard greens	8 cups
one 12-oz. pkg.	frozen corn kernels, thawed	two 12-oz. pkg.
one 10-oz. pkg.	frozen lima beans or frozen edamame, thawed	two 10-oz. pkg.
¾ cup	half-and-half or light cream	1½ cups
2 Tbsp.	snipped fresh sage	¼ cup
½ tsp.	salt	1 tsp.
¼ tsp.	black pepper	½ tsp.

Farmer's Salad

Cotija cheese is a tangy, salty, crumbly fresh Mexican cheese. If you can't find it, you can substitute feta.

1. In a large pot cook corn in a large amount of boiling salted water 5 to 7 minutes or until tender. Remove corn from pot. Add green beans to the boiling water; cook 3 to 4 minutes or just until crisp-tender. Drain beans in a colander; rinse with cold water and drain well. Cut corn from cobs.

2. In a large bowl combine corn, green beans, tomatoes, and red onion. Toss gently to combine.

3. For dressing, in a food processor or blender combine the next seven ingredients (through salt). Cover and process or blend until nearly smooth. Drizzle dressing over vegetables; toss to coat. Sprinkle with cheese. Serve immediately.

PER SERVING *175 cal., 13 g fat (2 g sat. fat), 5 mg chol., 71 mg sodium, 13 g carb., 3 g fiber, 4 g pro.*

PREP 35 minutes
COOK 8 minutes

10 servings	ingredients	20 servings
3	ears fresh sweet corn, husks and silks removed	6
1½ lb.	fresh green beans, trimmed	3 lb.
3 cups	grape tomatoes	6 cups
half	small red onion, thinly sliced	one
1 cup	snipped fresh cilantro	2 cups
½ cup	olive oil	1 cup
3	jalapeño peppers, stemmed, seeded, and chopped (tip, page 12)	6
¼ cup	chopped shallots	½ cup
3 Tbsp.	cider vinegar	⅓ cup + 2 tsp.
1½ tsp.	bottled minced roasted garlic	1 Tbsp.
¼ tsp.	salt	½ tsp.
½ cup	crumbled Cotija cheese	1 cup

Confetti Corn Salad

The "confetti" in this summery salad flavored with coconut, lime, turmeric, and cashews is created by a blend of yellow sweet corn, chopped cantaloupe, and chopped red sweet pepper.

1. Cut corn from cobs to equal 3 cups. For dressing, in a large bowl whisk together the next five ingredients (through salt). Add corn, red peppers, cantaloupe, and cashews. Toss to coat. Sprinkle with toasted coconut and, if desired, corn nuts.

FOR 20 SERVINGS In Step 1, cut about 6 cups corn.

*TIP Stir the coconut milk before measuring.

PER SERVING *177 cal., 11 g fat (4 g sat. fat), 0 mg chol., 204 mg sodium, 20 g carb., 3 g fiber, 5 g pro.*

START TO FINISH 30 minutes

10 servings	ingredients	20 servings
6	ears fresh corn, husks and silks removed	12
1 cup	canned unsweetened light coconut milk*	2 cups
1	green onion, thinly sliced	2
¼ cup	lime juice	½ cup
1 tsp.	ground turmeric	2 tsp.
½ tsp.	kosher salt	1 tsp.
2 cups	chopped red sweet pepper	4 cups
1 cup	chopped cantaloupe	2 cups
1 cup	roasted, salted cashews	2 cups
¼ cup	unsweetened coconut flakes, toasted (tip, page 19)	½ cup
½ cup	corn nuts (optional)	1 cup

Tex-Mex Potato Salad

Try a twist on traditional potato salad at your next picnic with this hearty combo of potatoes, celery, onion, black beans, corn, and hard-cooked eggs tossed in a smoky, spicy chipotle-infused dressing.

1. In a large saucepan combine potatoes, ¼ tsp. of the salt, and enough cold water to cover. Simmer, covered, 15 minutes or just until potatoes are tender; drain. Cool slightly.

2. Meanwhile, for dressing, in an extra-large bowl combine mayonnaise, ranch dressing, chipotle pepper, and remaining salt. Stir in celery and onion. Add potatoes, eggs, black beans, and corn; stir gently to coat. Cover and chill 6 to 24 hours. Serve with tortilla chips.

FOR 24 SERVINGS In Step 1, use ½ tsp. of the salt.

PER SERVING *300 cal., 21 g fat (4 g sat. fat), 104 mg chol., 536 mg sodium, 22 g carb., 3 g fiber, 7 g pro.*

PREP 40 minutes
CHILL 6 hours

12 servings	ingredients	24 servings
2 lb.	red and/or yellow new potatoes, quartered	4 lb.
¾ tsp.	salt	1½ tsp.
¾ cup	mayonnaise or salad dressing	1½ cups
¾ cup	bottled ranch salad dressing	1½ cups
1	canned chipotle chile pepper in adobo sauce, finely chopped (tip, page 12)	2
1 cup	thinly sliced celery	2 cups
⅓ cup	chopped onion	⅔ cup
6	hard-cooked eggs, coarsely chopped	12
1 cup	canned black beans, rinsed and drained	2 cups
1 cup	frozen corn, thawed	2 cups
	Tortilla chips	

Zucchini and Crispy Potato Salad

The popularity of vegetable slicers, or "spiralizers," has resulted in a wave of new ways to prepare vegetables, both cooked and raw. This salad is a yummy combination of crunchy fresh zucchini spirals, juicy cherry tomatoes, and crisp-baked potato shoestrings.

1. Preheat oven to 350°F. Line a baking sheet with nonstick foil. Coat foil with cooking spray.

2. For potato spirals, use a spiral vegetable slicer fitted with the chipper blade (large holes)* to cut potato into long strands. Snip spirals into 6- to 12-inch lengths and place in a large bowl. Drizzle with oil and sprinkle with salt and pepper; toss gently to coat. Place potato strands in a single layer on prepared baking sheet. Bake 15 to 20 minutes or until tender, stirring once. Increase oven temperature to 450°F. Bake 5 to 10 minutes more or until potato strands are golden brown and crisp.

3. Meanwhile, for zucchini spirals, use the spiral vegetable slicer fitted with the chipper blade (large holes)* to cut zucchini into long strands. Snip strands into 6- to 12-inch lengths. In a serving bowl combine zucchini strands, tomatoes, and basil.

4. For the dressing, in a bowl whisk together canola oil, vinegar, lemon juice, mustard, salt, and pepper. Pour dressing over salad; toss gently to coat. Top with potato spirals.

FOR 8 SERVINGS Use two baking sheets.

*TIP If you don't have a spiral vegetable slicer, for 4 servings, use 2 small potatoes. With a vegetable peeler, slice potatoes and zucchini lengthwise into thin, wide ribbons. Cut ribbons into about ¼-inch-wide strips, then continue as directed. For 8 servings, use 4 small potatoes.

PER SERVING *160 cal., 11 g fat (1 g sat. fat), 0 mg chol., 226 mg sodium, 15 g carb., 2 g fiber, 2 g pro.*

PREP 35 minutes
BAKE 15 minutes at 350°F + 5 min. at 450°F

4 servings	ingredients	8 servings
	Nonstick cooking spray	
1	large potato, peeled	2
1 Tbsp.	olive oil	2 Tbsp.
¼ tsp.	salt	½ tsp.
⅛ tsp.	black pepper	¼ tsp.
1	large zucchini	2
1 to 1½ cups	halved cherry tomatoes	2 to 3 cups
2 Tbsp.	snipped fresh basil, Italian parsley, or tarragon	¼ cup
2 Tbsp.	canola oil	¼ cup
2 tsp.	rice vinegar	4 tsp.
2 tsp.	fresh lemon juice	4 tsp.
1 tsp.	Dijon mustard	2 tsp.
⅛ tsp.	salt	¼ tsp.
⅛ tsp.	black pepper	¼ tsp.

Easy Hash Brown Bake

6 servings	ingredients	12 servings
2 Tbsp.	vegetable oil	¼ cup
half 32-oz. pkg.	loose-pack frozen diced hash brown potatoes	one 32-oz. pkg.
¼ cup	chopped onion	½ cup
half 10.75-oz. can	condensed cream of chicken soup	one 10.75-oz. can
one 8-oz. carton	light sour cream	two 8-oz. cartons
1 cup	diced cooked ham	2 cups
4 oz.	American cheese, cubed	8 oz.
⅛ tsp.	black pepper	¼ tsp.
1 cup	crushed cornflakes	2 cups
2 Tbsp.	butter or margarine, melted	¼ cup

This is the pinnacle of comfort food—hash browns, onion, and ham baked in a rich, cheesy sauce and topped with crisp, butter-tossed cornflakes. Take it to a potluck and it will be inhaled.

1. Preheat oven to 350°F. In a large ovenproof skillet heat oil over medium-high heat. Cook potatoes in hot oil 7 minutes. Stir in onion; cook 3 minutes or until some potatoes are lightly browned. Stir in soup, sour cream, ham, cheese, and pepper. Spoon into an 8×8-inch baking dish.

2. In a bowl stir together cornflakes and melted butter; sprinkle over hash browns. Bake, uncovered, 45 to 50 minutes or until hot and bubbly.

FOR 12 SERVINGS Use a 9×13-inch baking pan.

PER SERVING *366 cal., 22 g fat (10 g sat. fat), 58 mg chol., 1,002 mg sodium, 29 g carb., 2 g fiber, 13 g pro.*

Basil and Olive Potatoes

Oil infused with fresh basil and garlic forms the base of the dressing for this Mediterranean-inspired potato salad.

1. In a large pot cook potatoes in boiling salted water, covered, 10 minutes or just until tender; drain.

2. Meanwhile, for dressing, in a small saucepan combine oil, ½ cup of the basil, and the garlic; cook over medium-low heat 5 minutes. Remove basil from oil and discard. In a blender combine garlic-oil and the next five ingredients (through black pepper). Cover and blend until smooth. Transfer potatoes to a serving bowl. Pour dressing over potatoes and gently toss to coat; cover and set aside.

3. Grill sweet peppers, covered, over medium heat 7 to 10 minutes or until charred, turning occasionally. Cool slightly. Halve peppers; remove stems and seeds. Cut into large pieces. Add grilled pepper pieces and olives to potatoes; toss to coat. Add the remaining basil and toss again. Serve warm or at room temperature.

FOR 20 SERVINGS In Step 2, use 1 cup of the fresh basil.

PER SERVING *180 cal., 11 g fat (1 g sat. fat), 1 mg chol., 305 mg sodium, 19 g carb., 3 g fiber, 2 g pro.*

START TO FINISH 40 minutes

10 servings	ingredients	20 servings
2 lb.	small new potatoes, quartered	4 lb.
⅓ cup	canola oil	⅔ cup
1½ cups	fresh basil leaves	3 cups
3	cloves garlic, minced	6
⅓ cup	white wine vinegar	⅔ cup
2 Tbsp.	lemon juice	¼ cup
2 Tbsp.	mayonnaise	¼ cup
½ tsp.	salt	1 tsp.
½ tsp.	black pepper	1 tsp.
2	large yellow sweet peppers	4
1 cup	green olives, pitted	2 cups

Mexican Red Rice

Similar to classic Spanish red rice, this super-simple dish makes a nice accompaniment to grilled chicken, steak, or shrimp. Use a salsa that has a heat level that corresponds to your taste.

PREP 25 minutes
COOK 23 minutes
STAND 5 minutes

6 servings	ingredients	12 servings
1 Tbsp.	vegetable oil	2 Tbsp.
½ cup	chopped onion	1 cup
2	cloves garlic, minced	4
¼ tsp.	kosher salt	½ tsp.
1 cup	uncooked long grain rice	2 cups
one 14.5-oz. can	reduced-sodium chicken broth or vegetable broth	two 14.5-oz. cans
¾ cup	salsa	1½ cups
¼ cup	water	½ cup
½ cup	fresh cilantro leaves	1 cup

1. In a medium saucepan heat oil over medium-high heat. Add onion, garlic, and salt; cook 2 minutes. Stir in rice; cook and stir 1 minute. Add broth, salsa, and the water. Bring to boiling; reduce heat. Simmer, covered, 20 minutes or until rice is tender.

2. Remove saucepan from heat; remove lid. Cover saucepan with a clean kitchen towel; replace lid. Let stand 5 minutes to let the towel absorb excess moisture. Remove lid and towel. Add cilantro; fluff rice with a fork.

PER SERVING *166 cal., 4 g fat (0 g sat. fat), 0 mg chol., 323 mg sodium, 29 g carb., 1 g fiber, 4 g pro.*

Pear and Sweet Potato Soup

A slice of sautéed pear makes an elegant garnish for a special or holiday meal, but on a weeknight, you can certainly skip it. A drizzle of sour cream and a sprinkle of fresh thyme and cracked black pepper will do just fine.

1. In a large pot melt butter over medium-low heat. Add onion and garlic; cook and stir 5 minutes or until tender. Add pears, potatoes, salt, and thyme. Cook and stir 3 minutes more. Stir in broth. Bring to boiling; reduce heat.

2. Simmer, covered, 30 to 35 minutes or until tender. Using an immersion blender, blend until smooth. (Or carefully add soup in batches to a blender. Cover and blend until smooth.) Top with Sautéed Pear Slices, sour cream, fresh thyme sprigs, and cracked black pepper, if desired.

PER SERVING *168 cal., 4 g fat (2 g sat. fat), 10 mg chol., 810 mg sodium, 31 g carb., 5 g fiber, 4 g pro.*

*SAUTÉED PEAR SLICES Slice a pear vertically with stem and core intact; remove seeds. In a large skillet cook slices in 1 Tbsp. hot butter over medium-high heat 4 minutes or until golden brown, turning once. Drain slices on paper towels.

PREP 25 minutes **COOK** 35 minutes

6 servings	ingredients	12 servings
2 Tbsp.	butter	¼ cup
1 cup	chopped onion	2 cups
1	clove garlic, minced	2
4 cups	peeled and cored chopped pears	8 cups
1½ cups	peeled and chopped sweet potato	3 cups
1 cup	peeled and chopped russet potato	2 cups
1 tsp.	salt	2 tsp.
½ tsp.	chopped fresh thyme or pinch of dried thyme	1 tsp.
4 cups	reduced-sodium chicken broth	8 cups
	Sautéed Pear Slices*, sour cream, fresh thyme sprigs, cracked black pepper (optional)	

Savory Double-Walnut Scones

Finely ground walnuts act as a sort of "flour" in these buttermilk scones and help make them super tender. Tangy Gruyère cheese, thyme, honey, and Dijon mustard infuse them with amazing flavor.

1. Preheat oven to 350°F. Place walnuts on a baking sheet. Bake 7 to 9 minutes or until toasted. Coarsely chop 1 cup of the walnuts. Finely grind remaining walnuts; set aside. Increase oven temperature to 375°F.

2. In a large bowl combine flour, finely ground walnuts, baking powder, baking soda, and salt. Using a pastry blender, cut in butter until the mixture resembles coarse meal. Stir in Gruyère, the coarsely chopped walnuts, and thyme. Make a well in center of mixture. In a bowl combine egg, buttermilk, honey, and mustard; add all at once to flour mixture. Using a fork, stir just until moistened.

3. Turn dough out onto a lightly floured surface. Knead by folding and gently pressing 10 to 12 strokes or until nearly smooth. Divide in half. Pat or lightly roll each half to a ¾-inch-thick circle about 6 inches in diameter. Cut each circle into eight triangles. Place triangles 2 inches apart on greased baking sheet. Bake 18 to 20 minutes or until golden brown.

4. Transfer to cooling rack. If desired, top with additional cheese, walnuts, and thyme. Serve warm.

FOR 32 SERVINGS In Step 1, coarsely chop 2 cups of the toasted walnuts; finely grind remaining walnuts. In Step 4, divide dough into quarters. Pat or lightly roll each quarter to a ¾-inch-thick circle 6 inches in diameter. Continue as directed, using two greased baking sheets.

PER SERVING *220 cal., 15 g fat (6 g sat. fat), 37 mg chol., 229 mg sodium, 17 g carb., 1 g fiber, 6 g pro.*

PREP 20 minutes
BAKE 7 minutes at 350°F + 18 minutes at 375°F

16 servings	ingredients	32 servings
1¼ cups	walnuts	2½ cups
2¼ cups	all-purpose flour	4½ cups
2 tsp.	baking powder	4 tsp.
½ tsp.	baking soda	1 tsp.
¼ tsp.	salt	½ tsp.
½ cup	cold butter	1 cup
4 oz.	Gruyère cheese, shredded	8 oz.
½ tsp.	dried thyme, crushed	1 tsp.
1	egg, lightly beaten	2
1 cup	buttermilk	2 cups
1 Tbsp.	honey	2 Tbsp.
1 Tbsp.	Dijon mustard	2 Tbsp.

CHAPTER 6

Desserts

Sweets have the power to make any moment or occasion special. From a simple bar to an elegant and icy granita, you'll find what you're craving here.

163 Puffed Oven Pancake with Glazed Apples

164 Bananas Foster Bake

166 Grapefruit and Pear Crumble

168 Blackberry-Blueberry Cobbler

169 Stone Fruit-Coconut Crisp

171 Peach-Cardamom Slab Pie

172 Lemon Bar Ice Cream Sandwiches

173 Green Apple-Chardonnay Granita

174 Raspberry Fudge Pudding Cake

176 Blueberry-Lemonade Poke Cake

177 Gooey Chocolate-Caramel Cake

179 Banana Split Cake

180 Fresh Apple Snack Cake

182 Banana-Rum Bars

183 Tangy Apricot-Rosemary Bars with Pine Nut Streusel

185 Salted Peanut Butter and Chocolate Blondies

186 Butterscotch-Pretzel Bars

166

171

182

Puffed Oven Pancake with Glazed Apples

This is a lovely fall dessert—but it's also fun to make for a celebratory breakfast served with savory sage-infused sausage and good coffee.

1. Preheat oven to 400°F. Place the 1 Tbsp. butter in a 9×2-inch round baking dish. Place pan in oven 3 to 5 minutes or until butter is melted.

2. Meanwhile, in a bowl beat eggs with a wire whisk. Whisk in flour, milk, and salt until smooth. Immediately pour batter into the hot pan. Bake 20 to 25 minutes or until puffed and well browned.

3. Meanwhile, for glazed apples, in a large skillet melt the ¼ cup butter over medium heat; add apples. Cook and stir 8 minutes or until apples are tender. Stir in brown sugar; cook 1 to 2 minutes or until sauce is smooth, stirring gently. Remove skillet from heat. Carefully stir in rum. Return skillet to heat; heat through.

4. Serve glazed apples over pancake. If desired, sprinkle lightly with powdered sugar. Serve warm.

FOR 8 SERVINGS Use two 9×2-inch round baking dishes or one 9×13-inch baking pan. In Step 1, use 2 Tbsp. butter. In Step 3, use ½ cup butter.

PER SERVING *278 cal., 17 g fat (10 g sat. fat), 133 mg chol., 235 mg sodium, 24 g carb., 1 g fiber, 5 g pro.*

PREP 15 minutes
BAKE 20 minutes at 400°F

4 servings	ingredients	8 servings
1 Tbsp.	butter	2 Tbsp.
2	eggs	4
⅓ cup	all-purpose flour	⅔ cup
⅓ cup	milk	⅔ cup
⅛ tsp.	salt	¼ tsp.
¼ cup	butter, cut up	½ cup
1	medium cooking apple, cored, peeled, and thinly sliced	2
3 Tbsp.	packed brown sugar	⅓ cup
1 Tbsp.	light rum or apple juice	2 Tbsp.
	Powdered sugar (optional)	

Bananas Foster Bake

PREP 20 minutes
BAKE 25 minutes at 375°F
COOL 30 minutes

6 servings	ingredients	12 servings
½ cup	all-purpose flour	1 cup
½ cup	granulated sugar	1 cup
¾ tsp.	baking powder	1½ tsp.
¼ tsp.	salt	½ tsp.
¼ cup	butter, melted	½ tsp.
¼ cup	milk	½ cup
2 Tbsp.	dark rum or milk	¼ cup
½ tsp.	vanilla	1 tsp.
2	medium bananas, peeled and sliced lengthwise	4
¼ cup	raisins	½ cup
½ cup	rolled oats	1 cup
6 Tbsp.	packed brown sugar	¾ cup
¼ cup	all-purpose flour	½ cup
¼ cup	butter, cut up	½ cup
½ cup	chopped walnuts, pecans, or macadamia nuts	1 cup
	Vanilla bean ice cream (optional)	

Get a taste of New Orleans—the origin of Bananas Foster—with this simple oven version of the classic dessert that requires no flambéing.

1. Preheat oven to 375°F. Grease an 8×8-inch baking dish.

2. In a bowl stir together the first four ingredients (through salt); add melted butter, milk, rum, and vanilla. Stir until smooth. Spread batter in prepared baking dish. Top with sliced bananas and raisins.

3. In a large bowl combine oats, brown sugar, and the ¼ cup flour. Using a pastry blender, cut in cut-up butter until mixture resembles coarse crumbs. Stir in nuts. Sprinkle crumb mixture over batter.

4. Bake 25 to 30 minutes or until browned and set. Cool in pan on a wire rack 30 minutes. If desired, serve warm with ice cream.

FOR 8 SERVINGS For 12 servings, use a 9×13-inch baking dish. In Step 3, use ½ cup flour.

PER SERVING *437 cal., 20 g fat (10 g sat. fat), 42 mg chol., 290 mg sodium, 62 g carb., 3 g fiber, 4 g pro.*

Grapefruit and Pear Crumble

The unusual combination of grapefruit and pears works surprisingly well in this warm fruit dessert. The "crumble" is a crisp and buttery mixture of brown sugar, oats, flour, flaxseed meal, and roasted pumpkin seeds.

PREP 30 minutes
BAKE 30 minutes at 375°F

6 servings	ingredients	12 servings
	Nonstick cooking spray	
1	pear, peeled, cored, and thinly sliced	2
1 Tbsp.	all-purpose flour	2 Tbsp.
4	grapefruit, peeled, pith removed, and sliced	8
2 Tbsp.	chia seeds	¼ cup
½ cup	packed brown sugar	1 cup
½ cup	quick-cooking rolled oats	1 cup
¼ cup	all-purpose flour	½ cup
¼ cup	flaxseed meal	½ cup
¼ cup	coarsely chopped roasted salted pumpkin seeds (pepitas)	½ cup
½ cup	butter	1 cup
	Sweetened whipped cream or yogurt (optional)	

1. Preheat oven to 375°F. Lightly coat an 8×8-inch baking dish with cooking spray. Toss pear slices with 1 Tbsp. flour and arrange in the prepared dish. Top pears with half the grapefruit slices and sprinkle with half the chia seeds. Repeat with remaining grapefruit and chia seeds.

2. In a bowl combine the brown sugar, oats, the ¼ cup flour, flaxseed meal, and pumpkin seeds. Cut in butter until mixture starts to cling together. Sprinkle over fruit.

3. Bake 30 minutes or until crumble is bubbly and top is brown. Serve with whipped cream or yogurt if desired.

FOR 12 SERVINGS Use a 9×13-inch baking dish. In Step 1, toss pears with 2 Tbsp. flour. In Step 2, use ½ cup flour.

PER SERVING *436 cal., 24 g fat (11 g sat. fat), 41 mg chol., 166 mg sodium, 54 g carb., 8 g fiber, 8 g pro.*

Blackberry-Blueberry Cobbler

As desserts go, this beautiful purple number is fairly healthful. The biscuitlike bottom is made partially with whole wheat flour and it's loaded with fresh blackberries and blueberries.

PREP 25 minutes
BAKE 40 minutes at 350°F
COOL 30 minutes

6 servings	ingredients	12 servings
½ cup	all-purpose flour	1 cup
½ cup	whole wheat flour	1 cup
1 tsp.	baking powder	2 tsp.
⅛ tsp.	salt	¼ tsp.
¼ cup	butter, softened	½ cup
¾ cup	granulated sugar	1½ cups
⅓ cup	milk	⅔ cup
1½ cups	fresh blackberries	3 cups
¾ cup	fresh blueberries	1½ cups
¾ cup	water	1½ cups
	Powdered sugar (optional)	
	Ice cream or half-and-half (optional)	

1. Preheat oven to 350°F. Grease an 8×8-inch baking dish. In a bowl stir together the flours, baking powder, and salt.

2. In a large bowl beat butter with a mixer on medium to high for 30 seconds. Beat in ½ cup of the granulated sugar until fluffy. Alternately add flour mixture and milk to butter mixture, beating on low after each addition just until combined.

3. Spread batter in prepared baking dish. Top with blackberries and blueberries; sprinkle with remaining granulated sugar. Pour the water over fruit.

4. Bake 40 to 50 minutes or until a toothpick inserted in cake comes out clean. (Some fruit will sink toward bottom as cake rises.) Cool on a wire rack 30 minutes. Serve warm. If desired, sprinkle lightly with powdered sugar and serve with ice cream.

FOR 12 SERVINGS Use a 9×13-inch baking dish. In Step 2, use 1 cup of the granulated sugar.

PER SERVING *271 cal., 9 g fat (5 g sat. fat), 22 mg chol., 206 mg sodium, 47 g carb., 4 g fiber, 4 g pro.*

Stone Fruit-Coconut Crisp

Coconut adds a sweet and nutty dimension to the topping for this warming crisp. Use the stone fruit of your choice: peaches, nectarines, or plums—or a combination.

1. If using frozen cherries, let stand at room temperature 30 minutes (do not drain). Preheat oven to 375°F. Remove 1½ tsp. zest and squeeze ¼ cup juice from oranges. In a 2- to 4-qt. Dutch oven stir together granulated sugar and cornstarch. Stir in cherries, stone fruit, and orange juice. Cook and stir over medium heat until thickened and bubbly. Transfer to an 8×8-inch baking dish.

2. For topping, in a bowl stir together oats, brown sugar, flour, and orange zest. Using a pastry blender, cut in butter until mixture resembles coarse crumbs. Stir in coconut. Sprinkle topping over fruit mixture.

3. Bake 25 minutes or until fruit is tender and topping is golden. Serve warm and, if desired, with ice cream sprinkled with cinnamon.

FOR 8 SERVINGS Use a 4- to 6-qt. Dutch oven and a 9×13-inch baking dish. In Step 1, remove 1 Tbsp. zest and squeeze ½ cup juice from oranges.

PER SERVING *420 cal., 13 g fat (9 g sat. fat), 20 mg chol., 103 mg sodium, 74 g carb., 6 g fiber, 5 g pro.*

PREP 40 minutes
BAKE 25 minutes at 375°F

4 servings	ingredients	8 servings
2 cups	fresh or frozen pitted Royal Ann or dark sweet cherries	4 cups
1	orange	2
¼ cup	granulated sugar	½ cup
4½ tsp.	cornstarch	3 Tbsp.
3 cups	sliced stone fruit, such as nectarines, plums, and/or peeled peaches	6 cups
⅓ cup	rolled oats	⅔ cup
¼ cup	packed brown sugar	½ cup
3 Tbsp.	all-purpose flour	6 Tbsp.
3 Tbsp.	butter, cut up	6 Tbsp.
½ cup	flaked coconut	1 cup
	Coconut or vanilla ice cream (optional)	
	Ground cinnamon (optional)	

Peach-Cardamom Slab Pie

Slab pies have grown in popularity in recent years. They're easier to assemble than a traditional round pie—and they feed a big crowd. This one calls for a puff pastry crust—especially easy and light.

1. Preheat oven to 400°F. Line a 15×10-inch baking pan with parchment paper or foil. On a lightly floured surface, unfold pastry. Roll into a 15×12-inch rectangle. Transfer pastry to prepared pan.

2. Remove 1 tsp. zest and squeeze 1 Tbsp. juice from lemon. In a bowl stir together granulated sugar, cornstarch, half the lemon zest, the lemon juice, and cardamom. Add peach slices; toss gently to coat. Spoon crosswise onto half the pastry rectangle, spreading to within 1 inch of edges. Combine egg and the water; brush some on uncovered pastry edges.

3. Fold uncovered pastry half over peach mixture. Using a fork, firmly press edges of pastry together to seal. Brush pastry with remaining egg wash. Cut two or three slits in top pastry. Bake 25 to 30 minutes or until pastry is golden and filling is bubbly. Cool on a wire rack.

4. For icing, in a bowl stir together powdered sugar, butter, and remaining lemon zest. Stir in enough milk to reach drizzling consistency. Drizzle icing over pastry. Cut into narrow wedges.

FOR 32 SERVINGS Use two 15×10-inch baking pans. In Step 2, remove 2 tsp. zest and squeeze 2 Tbsp. juice from lemon.

PER SERVING *147 cal., 7 g fat (2 g sat. fat), 14 mg chol., 49 mg sodium, 20 g carb., 0 g fiber, 2 g pro.*

PREP 30 minutes
BAKE 25 minutes at 400°F

16 servings	ingredients	32 servings
half 17.3-oz. pkg.	frozen puff pastry sheets, thawed	one 17.3-oz. pkg.
1	lemon	1
⅓ cup	granulated sugar	⅔ cup
1 Tbsp.	cornstarch	2 Tbsp.
one 16-oz. pkg.	frozen unsweetened peach slices, thawed, drained, and chopped	two 16-oz. pkg.
½ tsp.	cardamom	1 tsp.
1	egg, lightly beaten	2
1 Tbsp.	water	2 Tbsp.
¾ cup	powdered sugar	1½ cups
1 Tbsp.	butter, softened	2 Tbsp.
4 to 5 tsp.	milk	8 to 10 tsp.

Lemon Bar Ice Cream Sandwiches

How do you make lemon bars even better? Fill them with vanilla ice cream swirled with lemon curd and lemon zest, of course! Crushed lemon drops are a lip-puckering (and optional) addition.

PREP 55 minutes
BAKE 10 minutes per batch at 350°F
FREEZE 4 hours

20 servings	ingredients	40 servings
6 Tbsp.	butter, softened	¾ cup
¾ cup	sugar	1½ cups
2 tsp.	lemon zest	4 tsp.
¼ tsp. + ⅛ tsp.	baking soda	¾ tsp.
¼ tsp. + ⅛ tsp.	cream of tartar	¾ tsp.
¼ tsp.	salt	½ tsp.
1	egg	2
½ tsp.	vanilla	1 tsp.
1 cup + 2 Tbsp.	all-purpose flour	2¼ cups
half 1.75-qt. container (3½ cups)	vanilla ice cream	one 1.75-qt. container (7 cups)
¾ cup	purchased lemon curd	1½ cups
1½ tsp.	lemon zest	1 Tbsp.
	Crushed lemon drops (optional)	

1. Preheat oven to 350°F. Line an 8×8-inch baking pan with foil, extending foil over edges of pan. In a large bowl beat butter with a mixer on medium to high 30 seconds. Add the next five ingredients (through salt). Beat until combined, scraping sides of bowl occasionally. Beat in egg and vanilla until combined. Beat in as much of the flour as you can with the mixer. Stir in any remaining flour.

2. Press half the dough onto bottom of prepared baking pan. Bake 10 to 12 minutes or until lightly browned. Cool in pan on a wire rack 5 minutes. Use foil to lift cookie out of pan; cool on a wire rack. Cool pan; line with foil. Repeat with remaining dough.

3. Place ice cream in an extra-large bowl; stir until softened and spreadable. Add lemon curd and lemon zest; fold gently to swirl. Peel foil from cookies. Line the cooled baking pan with plastic wrap, extending wrap over edges of pan. Place one cookie in pan. Spread with ice cream mixture; top with remaining cookie. Cover and freeze at least 4 hours or until firm. Use plastic wrap to lift ice cream sandwiches out of pan. Cut into rectangles. If desired, sprinkle sides of sandwiches with crushed candies.

FOR 40 SERVINGS Use a 9×13-inch baking pan.

TO MAKE AHEAD Wrap sandwiches individually with plastic wrap, then place in an airtight container; cover. Freeze up to 1 month.

PER SERVING *173 cal., 7 g fat (4 g sat. fat), 37 mg chol., 109 mg sodium, 27 g carb., 2 g fiber, 2 g pro.*

Green Apple-Chardonnay Granita

When the weather is hot—or you've just eaten a rich, heavy dinner—this cold, refreshing, and light-as-can-be dessert is a fitting way to finish the meal.

1. In a bowl stir together wine and sugar until sugar is completely dissolved.

2. In a food processor or blender combine apples, ½ cup of the apple juice, and the lemon juice. Cover and process until smooth. Press mixture through a fine-mesh sieve, reserving liquid. Discard pulp. Add enough of the remaining apple juice to strained liquid to equal 2½ cups. Stir in wine mixture.

3. Transfer mixture to a 9×13-inch baking dish. Freeze 1½ hours or until slushy. Stir with a fork; freeze 1½ to 2 hours more or until set. Using a fork, scrape granita into flakes. If desired, serve with thinly sliced apple.

FOR 16 SERVINGS In Step 2, use 1 cup of the apple juice. Add enough apple juice to strained liquid to equal 5 cups. In Step 3, use two 9×13-inch baking dishes.

TO MAKE AHEAD Prepare as directed, except do not scrape into flakes with a fork. Cover with plastic wrap, then heavy foil. Freeze up to 1 month. Scrape into flakes as directed.

PER SERVING *109 cal., 0 g fat, 0 mg chol., 4 mg sodium, 22 g carb., 2 g fiber, 0 g pro.*

PREP 20 minutes
FREEZE 3 hours

8 servings	ingredients	16 servings
1 cup	Chardonnay or other dry white wine	2 cups
⅓ cup	superfine sugar	⅔ cup
1⅓ cups	chopped Granny Smith apples	2⅔ cups
1½ cups	apple juice	3 cups
2 Tbsp.	fresh lemon juice	¼ cup
	Thinly sliced Granny Smith apple (optional)	

Raspberry Fudge Pudding Cake

Raspberries and chocolate are natural partners. They come together beautifully in this warm, gooey pudding cake. If you don't want to bother with the sweetened whipped cream topping, vanilla ice cream works equally well.

PREP 30 minutes
BAKE 40 minutes at 350°F
COOL 1 hour

6 servings	ingredients	12 servings
two 10-oz. pkg.	frozen red raspberries in syrup, thawed	four 10-oz. pkg.
½ cup	all-purpose flour	1 cup
3 Tbsp.	unsweetened cocoa powder	6 Tbsp.
1 tsp.	baking powder	2 tsp.
2 Tbsp.	butter, softened	¼ cup
½ cup	packed brown sugar	1 cup
1 tsp.	vanilla	2 tsp.
¼ cup	milk	½ cup
⅓ cup	packed brown sugar	⅔ cup
⅔ cup	heavy cream	1⅓ cups
2 Tbsp.	sugar	¼ cup
1 tsp.	vanilla	2 tsp.
	Vanilla ice cream (optional)	

1. Preheat oven to 350°F. Grease an 8×8-inch baking dish. Drain raspberries, reserving ¾ cup syrup.

2. In a bowl stir together flour, 1 Tbsp. of the cocoa powder, and baking powder. In a bowl beat butter with a mixer on medium for 30 seconds. Beat in the ½ cup brown sugar and the vanilla. Add flour mixture and milk alternately, beating on low after each addition until combined.

3. Spread batter in prepared dish. Top with raspberries and drizzle with syrup. In a bowl stir together the ⅓ cup brown sugar and remaining cocoa powder; sprinkle over batter.

4. Bake 40 minutes or until a toothpick inserted ½ inch into cake portion comes out clean. Cool in pan on a wire rack 1 hour.

5. Meanwhile, for sweetened whipped cream, in a chilled bowl with chilled beaters beat cream, sugar, and vanilla on medium until soft peaks form. Serve cake warm with sweetened whipped cream or vanilla ice cream.

FOR 12 SERVINGS Use a 9×13-inch baking dish. In Step 2, use 2 Tbsp. of the cocoa powder and 1 cup brown sugar. In Step 3, use ⅔ cup brown sugar.

PER SERVING *367 cal., 5 g fat (2 g sat. fat), 12 mg chol., 114 mg sodium, 79 g carb., 3 g fiber, 3 g pro.*

Blueberry-Lemonade Poke Cake

"Poke" cakes are just what they sound like. While still warm from the oven, holes are poked into the cake with a wooden spoon handle so a sauce or syrup can drip through the center of it.

PREP 20 minutes
BAKE 25 minutes at 350°F
COOL 2 hours

24 servings	ingredients	48 servings
1 pkg.	2-layer-size white cake mix	2 pkg.
1 cup	buttermilk	2 cups
4	eggs	8
⅓ cup	canola oil	⅔ cup
1 Tbsp.	lemon zest	2 Tbsp.
½ tsp.	almond extract	1 tsp.
⅓ cup	sugar	⅔ cup
1 tsp.	cornstarch	2 tsp.
¼ cup	water	½ cup
2 cups	fresh or frozen blueberries	4 cups
½ cup	frozen lemonade concentrate, thawed	1 cup
one 8-oz. container	frozen whipped dessert topping, thawed	one 16-oz. container
½ cup	lemon curd	1 cup
	Quartered lemon slices (optional)	

1. Preheat oven to 350°F. Grease a 9×13-inch baking pan.

2. In a bowl combine the first six ingredients (through almond extract). Beat with a mixer on low just until combined. Beat on medium 2 minutes, scraping bowl occasionally. Spread batter into prepared baking pan.

3. Bake 25 to 30 minutes or until a toothpick inserted in cake comes out clean. Cool cake 5 minutes.

4. Meanwhile, prepare blueberry sauce. In a medium saucepan combine sugar and cornstarch. Add water, mix well. Add blueberries. Cook and stir over medium heat until mixture is slightly thickened and bubbly. Cook and stir 2 minutes more. Mash with a potato masher or fork (sauce will not be completely smooth).

5. Using the handle of a wooden spoon, poke holes into cake about 1 inch apart. Drizzle and brush lemonade concentrate over cake. Spread blueberry sauce over cake. Cool completely.

6. In a large bowl stir a small amount of whipped topping into lemon curd to lighten. Fold in remaining whipped topping. Spread over cake. If desired, top servings with a lemon slice. Cover and refrigerate leftovers up to 24 hours.

FOR 48 SERVINGS Use two 9×13-inch baking pans.

PER SERVING *207 cal., 7 g fat (3 g sat. fat), 37 mg chol., 173 mg sodium, 32 g carb., 1 g fiber, 3 g pro.*

Gooey Chocolate-Caramel Cake

The combination of chocolate cake with caramel topping makes this the cake form of chocolate-covered English toffee. (And, in fact, a sprinkling of chopped English toffee tops it off!)

1. Preheat oven to 350°F. Grease and lightly flour a 9×13-inch baking pan.

2. Prepare cake mix according to package directions. Pour into prepared pan. Bake according to package directions. Cool cake in pan on a wire rack.

3. Using the handle of a wooden spoon, poke holes into cake about 1 inch apart. Slowly pour sweetened condensed milk over cake, then slowly pour caramel topping over cake. Serve with whipped topping and sprinkle with chopped toffee.

FOR 60 SERVINGS Use two 9×13-inch baking pans.

TO MAKE AHEAD Prepare as directed, except do not sprinkle with chopped toffee. Cover and refrigerate cake up to 24 hours. Before serving, sprinkle with chopped toffee.

PER SERVING *186 cal., 5 g fat (3 g sat. fat), 6 mg chol., 197 mg sodium, 33 g carb., 1 g fiber, 2 g pro.*

PREP 15 minutes
BAKE 26 minutes at 350°F
COOL 2 hours

30 servings	ingredients	60 servings
1 pkg.	2-layer-size German chocolate cake mix	2 pkg.
one 14-oz. can	sweetened condensed milk	two 14-oz. cans
one 12-oz. jar	caramel-flavor ice cream topping	two 12-oz. jars
one 8-oz. container	frozen whipped dessert topping, thawed	one 16-oz. containers
three 1.4-oz. bars	chocolate-covered English toffee, chopped	six 1.4-oz. bars

Banana Split Cake

A classic ice cream-shop treat takes the form of a banana-strawberry swirl cake topped with chocolate sauce and fresh berries.

1. Preheat oven to 350°F. Grease and flour an 8×8-inch baking pan. In a bowl stir together flour, baking powder, salt, and baking soda.

2. In a large bowl beat butter with a mixer on medium to high 30 seconds. Gradually add sugar, ¼ cup at a time. Add eggs, one at a time, beating until combined after each addition. In a small bowl combine banana, sour cream, milk, and vanilla. Alternately add flour mixture and banana mixture to butter mixture, beating on low after each addition just until combined.

3. In another bowl stir together ½ cup of the batter, the strawberry preserves, and 1 or 2 drops red food coloring. In another bowl stir together another ½ cup of the batter and the cocoa powder. Spread remaining plain batter into prepared pan. Randomly spoon chocolate and strawberry batters in small mounds over plain batter. Use a table knife to gently swirl batters.

4. Bake 40 to 45 minutes or until a toothpick inserted in cake comes out clean. Cool completely in pan on a wire rack.

5. Before serving, in a small saucepan heat ice cream topping just to drizzling consistency. Drizzle topping over each serving. If desired, top with strawberries.

FOR 16 SERVINGS Use a 9×13-inch baking pan. In Step 3, stir together 1 cup batter, strawberry preserves, and a few drops of red food coloring. In another bowl stir together 1 cup batter and cocoa powder.

PER SERVING *414 cal., 17 g fat (9 g sat. fat), 81 mg chol., 382 mg sodium, 61 g carb., 1 g fiber, 6 g pro.*

PREP 40 minutes
BAKE 40 minutes at 350°F
COOL 2 hours

8 servings	ingredients	16 servings
1½ cups	all-purpose flour	3 cups
1 tsp.	baking powder	2 tsp.
½ tsp.	salt	1 tsp.
⅛ tsp.	baking soda	¼ tsp.
½ cup	butter, softened	1 cup
¾ cup	sugar	1½ cups
2	eggs, room temperature	4
¼ cup	mashed ripe banana	½ cup
¼ cup	sour cream	½ cup
¼ cup	milk	½ cup
½ tsp.	vanilla	1 tsp.
¼ cup	strawberry preserves	½ cup
	Red food coloring	
¼ cup	presweetened cocoa powder (not low-calorie)	½ cup
½ cup	chocolate fudge ice cream topping	1 cup
	Fresh strawberries (optional)	

Fresh Apple Snack Cake

Snack cakes are the culinary opposite of fancy layer cakes. They're easier to make than cookies but can be enjoyed in the same context—with a glass of milk after school or with a cup of tea in the evening.

PREP 30 minutes
BAKE 50 minutes at 350°F
COOL 1 hour

10 servings	ingredients	20 servings
1½ cups	all-purpose flour	3 cups
1 cup	sugar	2 cups
½ tsp.	baking soda	1 tsp.
½ tsp.	salt	1 tsp.
½ tsp.	ground cinnamon	1 tsp.
1	egg, lightly beaten	2
¼ cup + 2 Tbsp.	canola oil	¾ cup
1 tsp.	vanilla	2 tsp.
1½ cups	chopped, peeled Granny Smith apples	3 cups
½ cup	chopped pecans or walnuts, toasted (tip, page 19)	1 cup
	Whipped cream (optional)	

1. Preheat oven to 350°F. Grease an 8×8-inch baking pan. In a large bowl combine the first five ingredients (through cinnamon). Make a well in center of flour mixture.

2. In another bowl combine eggs, oil, and vanilla. Stir in apples and nuts. Add egg mixture to flour mixture, stirring just until moistened (batter will be thick). Spread batter into prepared pan.

3. Bake 50 to 55 minutes or until a toothpick comes out clean. Cool in pan on a wire rack 1 hour. Serve slightly warm or cool completely. If desired, serve with whipped cream.

FOR 20 SERVINGS Use a 9×13-inch baking pan.

PER SERVING *324 cal., 18 g fat (2 g sat. fat), 21 mg chol., 187 mg sodium, 38 g carb., 2 g fiber, 3 g pro.*

Banana-Rum Bars

When you can't decide between pie and cake, these tropically themed bars are a combination of the two. A moist banana cake sits atop a cinnamon-flavor pastry crust and is topped with a rum-infused cream cheese frosting.

1. Preheat oven to 350°F. For crust, in a large bowl beat ½ cup of the butter with a mixer on medium to high 30 seconds. Add granulated sugar and ¼ tsp. of the vanilla. Beat until combined, scraping sides of bowl occasionally. Beat in 1 cup of the flour, the cinnamon, and ¼ tsp. of the salt. Press mixture into an ungreased 8×8-inch baking pan. Bake 15 to 20 minutes or until light brown. Cool in pan on a wire rack.

2. In another large bowl beat remaining butter on medium to high 30 seconds. Add brown sugar, baking soda, and remaining salt. Beat until combined, scraping sides of bowl occasionally. Beat in eggs, bananas, rum, and remaining vanilla. Beat in remaining flour just until combined. Spread over baked crust.

3. Bake 40 to 45 minutes or until a toothpick inserted near center comes out clean. Cool in pan on wire rack. Spread cinnamon-rum frosting over cooled uncut bars. Lightly sprinkle with additional cinnamon. Cut into bars.

4. For cinnamon-rum frosting, in a bowl beat butter and cream cheese with a mixer on medium until combined and fluffy. Gradually beat in powdered sugar, cinnamon, and vanilla or rum.

FOR 36 SERVINGS Use a 9×13-inch baking pan. In Step 1, use 1 cup of the butter and ½ tsp. of the vanilla. Beat in 2 cups of the flour, the cinnamon, and ½ tsp. of the salt.

*NOTE If desired, for 18 servings, use 1½ tsp. milk and a dash of rum extract in place of rum. For 36 servings, use 1 Tbsp. milk and ⅛ tsp. rum extract.

PER SERVING *259 cal., 12 g fat (7 g sat. fat), 47 mg chol., 173 mg sodium, 40 g carb., 1 g fiber, 2 g pro.*

PREP 35 minutes
BAKE 55 minute at 350°F

18 servings	ingredients	36 servings
¾ cup	butter, softened	1½ cups
¼ cup	granulated sugar	½ cup
¾ tsp.	vanilla	1½ tsp.
2 cups	all-purpose flour	4 cups
½ tsp.	ground cinnamon	1 tsp.
¼ tsp. + ⅛ tsp.	salt	¾ tsp.
1 cup	packed brown sugar	2 cups
½ tsp.	baking soda	1 tsp.
2	eggs	3
¾ cup	mashed banana	1½ cups
1 Tbsp.	rum*	2 Tbsp.
¼ cup	butter, softened	½ cup
1½ oz.	cream cheese, softened	3 oz.
1½ cups	powdered sugar	3 cups
½ tsp.	ground cinnamon	¼ tsp.
1 Tbsp.	vanilla or rum	2 Tbsp.

Tangy Apricot-Rosemary Bars with Pine Nut Streusel

Bar cookies are naturally casual food because they're easy to make, but these herbed apricot bars with a pine nut streusel are decidedly elegant.

1. Preheat oven to 350°F. Line an 8×8-inch baking pan with foil, extending foil over edges of pan. Lightly grease foil.

2. For crust, in a large bowl stir together flour, ½ cup of the granulated sugar, the rosemary, baking powder, and ½ tsp. of the salt. Using a pastry blender, cut in ½ cup butter until mixture resembles coarse crumbs. Remove ¾ cup crumb mixture for streusel topping. Press remaining mixture into prepared baking pan. Bake 10 to 12 minutes or until set.

3. Meanwhile, for filling, drain apricots, reserving 2 Tbsp. syrup. In a saucepan combine apricots, reserved syrup, remaining granulated sugar, the water, cornstarch, the 1 Tbsp. butter, and remaining salt. Cook and stir over medium heat until thickened and bubbly. Cook and stir 1 minute more. Spoon apricot filling over hot crust. Combine streusel topping and pine nuts; sprinkle over apricot filling.

4. Bake 30 minutes more or until filling is bubbly around the edges and streusel is lightly browned. Cool in pan on a wire rack.

5. For icing, in a bowl stir together powdered sugar and vanilla. Stir in enough milk, 1 tsp. at a time, to reach drizzling consistency. Drizzle icing over uncut bars. Let stand until icing is set. Use foil to lift uncut bars out of pan; cut into bars.

FOR 32 SERVINGS Use a 9×13-inch baking pan. In Step 2, use 1 cup of the granulated sugar and 1 tsp. of the salt. Cut in 1 cup butter. Remove 1½ cups for streusel topping. In Step 3, reserve ¼ cup syrup and use 2 Tbsp. butter.

PER SERVING *181 cal., 7 g fat (4 g sat. fat), 17 mg chol., 165 mg sodium, 28 g carb., 1 g fiber, 2 g pro.*

PREP 40 minutes
BAKE 40 minutes at 350°F

16 servings	ingredients	32 servings
1½ cups	all-purpose flour	3 cups
¾ cup + 2 Tbsp.	granulated sugar	1¾ cups
1 tsp.	snipped fresh rosemary	2 tsp.
½ tsp.	baking powder	1 tsp.
½ tsp. + ⅛ tsp.	salt	1¼ tsp.
½ cup	butter, cut up	1 cup
one 15-oz. can	unpeeled apricot halves in light syrup, undrained	two 15-oz. cans
2½ Tbsp.	cold water	5 Tbsp.
1 Tbsp.	cornstarch	2 Tbsp.
1 Tbsp.	butter	2 Tbsp.
3 Tbsp.	pine nuts	⅓ cup
½ cup	powdered sugar	1 cup
⅛ tsp.	vanilla	¼ tsp.
1 to 2 Tbsp.	milk	2 to 4 Tbsp.

Salted Peanut Butter and Chocolate Blondies

Two old friends—peanut butter and chocolate—come together in a new way in these peanut-studded bars. A sprinkle of flaked sea salt over the chocolate offers a modern touch.

1. Preheat oven to 350°F. Line an 8×8-inch baking pan with foil, extending foil over edges of pan. Lightly coat foil with cooking spray. In a saucepan melt butter and peanut butter over medium heat. Stir in brown sugar. Stir in egg and vanilla until combined. Stir in flour, baking powder, and baking soda until combined. Stir in peanuts. Pat the dough into the prepared baking pan.

2. Bake 18 minutes. Top with the broken chocolate squares. Bake 2 minutes more or until evenly brown and edges are puffed. Sprinkle with sea salt. Cool in pan on a wire rack. Use edges of foil to lift uncut bars out of pan; cut into bars.

FOR 36 SERVINGS Use a 9×13-inch baking dish.

PER SERVING *157 cal., 7 g fat (3 g sat. fat), 18 mg chol., 147 mg sodium, 21 g carb., 1 g fiber, 3 g pro.*

PREP 25 minutes
BAKE 20 minutes at 350°F

18 servings	ingredients	36 servings
	Nonstick cooking spray	
¼ cup	butter, cut up	½ cup
3 Tbsp.	creamy peanut butter	⅓ cup
1 cup	packed brown sugar	2 cups
1	egg, lightly beaten	2
1 tsp.	vanilla	2 tsp.
1 cup	all-purpose flour	2 cups
½ tsp.	baking powder	1 tsp.
⅛ tsp.	baking soda	¼ tsp.
½ cup	salted and roasted peanuts, chopped	1 cup
half 5.25-oz. pkg.	dark chocolate squares or dark chocolate & sea salt caramel squares, broken into large pieces	one 5.25-oz. pkg.
	Flaked sea salt	

Butterscotch-Pretzel Bars

Fans of sweet and salty flavors, it doesn't get much better than this. The combination of a creamy butterscotch filling over a crunchy peanut butter-flavor pretzel crust—and a topping of crushed pretzels and peanuts—is absolutely irresistible.

PREP 25 minutes
CHILL 2 hours

18 servings	ingredients	36 servings
	Nonstick cooking spray	
¾ cup	powdered sugar	1½ cups
½ cup	creamy peanut butter	1 cup
3 Tbsp.	butter, melted	6 Tbsp.
1 cup	crushed pretzels	2 cups
half 11-oz. pkg.	butterscotch-flavor pieces	one 11-oz. pkg.
1 cup	heavy cream	2 cups
¼ cup	coarsely crushed pretzels	½ cup
¼ cup	chopped peanuts	½ cup

1. Line an 8×8-inch baking pan with foil, extending foil over edges of pan. Lightly coat foil with cooking spray. For crust, in a large bowl combine powdered sugar, peanut butter, and melted butter. Stir in the 1 cup crushed pretzels. Press onto bottom of prepared pan.

2. For filling, in a medium-size heavy saucepan stir butterscotch pieces and cream over low heat just until butterscotch pieces are melted.

3. Spread filling over crust. Sprinkle with coarsely crushed pretzels and peanuts; press lightly. Cover and chill until firm (at least 2 hours). Using foil, lift uncut bars out of pan. Cut into bars.

FOR 36 SERVINGS Use a 9×13-inch baking pan. In Step 2, stir in 2 cups of the crushed pretzels.

PER SERVING *166 cal., 10 g fat (5 g sat. fat), 7 mg chol., 154 mg sodium, 17 g carb., 1 g fiber, 3 g pro.*

Index

A

Appetizers and snacks
Baby Potatoes Roasted in Salt, 17
Bacon-Filled Medjool Dates, 19
Bacon-Stuffed Mushrooms, 8
Baked Tomato-Mozzarella Spread, 21
Barbecue-Spiced Roasted
   Chickpeas, 24
Cheesy Snack Mix, 25
Chicken and Eggplant Stuffed Shells, 6
Classic Nachos, 16
Fire-Roasted Tomato Salsa, 23
Fried Pickled Peppers with Ginger
   Aïoli, 12
Ham Balls in Barbecue Sauce, 9
Korean Beef Lettuce Wraps, 11
Picadillo Poppers, 13
Pizza Dip, 22
Prosciutto-Basil Cheese Balls, 20
Salmon and Cheese Stuffed
   Mushrooms, 8
Sriracha Deviled Eggs, 18
Stuffed Fresh Sweet Peppers, 14

Apples
Fresh Apple Snack Cake, 180
Green Apple-Chardonnay Granita, 173
Puffed Oven Pancake with Glazed
   Apples, 163
Apricot-Rosemary Bars with Pine Nut
   Streusel, Tangy, 183

Artichokes
Overgrown Garden Turkey Melt, 65
Smoky Pizza Melts, 102

Arugula
Chicken Paillard Salad, 31
Lemony Tuna Salad, 121
Asian Braising Sauce, 90
Asparagus and Penne Salad, 136

Avocados
Chicken Paillard Salad, 31
Stuffed Fresh Sweet Peppers, 14

B

Baby Potatoes Roasted in Salt, 17
Bacon
Bacon-Filled Medjool Dates, 19
Bacon-Stuffed Mushrooms, 8
Creamy Alfredo with Bacon and
   Peas, 97
Harvest Succotash, 146
Baked Curried Chicken with
   Cauliflower, 32
Baked Shrimp and Rice, 125
Baked Tomato-Mozzarella Spread, 21

Bananas
Banana-Rum Bars, 182
Banana Split Cake, 179
Bananas Foster Bake, 164

Bar cookies
Banana-Rum Bars, 182
Butterscotch-Pretzel Bars, 186
Lemon Bar Ice Cream Sandwiches, 172
Salted Peanut Butter and Chocolate
   Blondies, 185
Tangy Apricot-Rosemary Bars with
   Pine Nut Streusel, 183
Barbecue-Spiced Roasted
   Chickpeas, 24
Basil and Olive Potatoes, 155
Basil Halibut with Jalapeño Butter, 111
Basil Shrimp Chowder, 129

Beans. *See also* Edamame; Green
   beans; Lima beans
Barbecue-Spiced Roasted
   Chickpeas, 24
Butter Beans, Italian Sausage, and
   Chard, 53
Classic Nachos, 16
Pork Cassoulet, 88
Tex-Mex Potato Salad, 149

Beef
Beef Stew Pot Pie, 73
Brunswick Stew, 74
Classic Nachos, 16
Espresso-Marinated Flank Steak, 70
Ham Balls in Barbecue Sauce, 9
Italian Roast Beef Slider Melts, 77
Korean Beef Lettuce Wraps, 11
Mini Meat Loaves with Potatoes and
   Beans, 81
Orange Teriyaki Beef Stew, 75
Picadillo Poppers, 13
Steak with Spicy Balsamic Glaze, 72
Tacos in Pasta Shells, 78
Blackberry-Blueberry Cobbler, 168
Blueberry-Lemonade Poke Cake, 176

Bok choy
Orange Teriyaki Beef Stew, 75
Spicy Shrimp with Cabbage-Noodle
   Slaw, 127

Breads
Egg Baguette Bake, 99
Savory Double-Walnut Scones, 159

Broccoli
Chicken and Broccoli Stir-Fry, 35
Coconut-Curry Noodle Bowl, 50
Korean Beef Lettuce Wraps, 11
Lemon-Herb Roasted Salmon with
   Broccoli and Tomatoes, 115
Brunswick Stew, 74

Brussels sprouts
Pork Chops with Roasted Vegetables
   and Balsamic Drizzle, 82
Shaved Brussels Sprouts with Green
   Onion Vinaigrette, 138
Warm Brussels Sprouts Salad with
   Chicken, 45

Buffalo Chicken Rolls, 62
Butter Beans, Italian Sausage, and
   Chard, 53
Butterscotch-Pretzel Bars, 186

C

Cabbage
Peanutty Noodle Slaw, 137
Roasted Cabbage with Pears, 141
Spicy Asian Pork Cabbage Rolls, 90
Spicy Shrimp with Cabbage-Noodle
   Slaw, 127
Zesty Green Bean Slaw, 145
Cajun Sausage-Potato Soup, 103

Cakes
Banana Split Cake, 179
Blueberry-Lemonade Poke Cake, 176
Fresh Apple Snack Cake, 180
Gooey Chocolate-Caramel Cake, 177

Cantaloupe
Confetti Corn Salad, 148

Capocollo
Penne and Asparagus Salad, 136
Carrots, Spice-and-Honey Roasted, 143

Cauliflower
Baked Curried Chicken with
   Cauliflower, 32
Chicken Alfredo Cauliflower Rice
   Bake, 49

Cheese
Bacon-Stuffed Mushrooms, 8
Baked Tomato-Mozzarella Spread, 21
Cheesy Snack Mix, 25
Classic Nachos, 16
Egg Baguette Bake, 99
Picadillo Poppers, 13
Prosciutto-Basil Cheese Balls, 20
Salmon and Cheese Stuffed
   Mushrooms, 8

Cherries
Stone Fruit-Coconut Crisp, 169

Chia seeds
Grapefruit and Pear Crumble, 166

Chicken. *See also* Chicken sausages
Baked Curried Chicken with
   Cauliflower, 32
Buffalo Chicken Rolls, 62
Chicken Alfredo Cauliflower Rice
   Bake, 49
Chicken and Broccoli Stir-Fry, 35
Chicken and Eggplant Stuffed Shells, 6
Chicken and Spinach Phyllo Bake, 55
Chicken Caesar Lasagna, 33
Chicken Fajitas in a Flash, 38
Chicken Marsala Skillet, 36
Chicken Paillard Salad, 31
Chicken Tortilla Soup, 59
Coconut-Curry Noodle Bowl, 50
Creamy Chicken Enchiladas, 30

Curried Chicken Salad, 39
Greek Chicken and Pita Casserole, 46
Greek Chicken Kabobs, 48
Honey-Sriracha Grilled Chicken
    Thighs, 51
Italian Roasted Chicken and
    Vegetable Toss, 40
Mexican Corn-Chicken Casserole, 43
Nacho Chicken Drummettes, 52
Peanut Chicken Satay Stir-Fry, 44
Rosemary and Ravioli Chicken
    Soup, 56
Sweet-Spicy Barbecue Chicken
    Sliders, 61
Warm Brussels Sprouts Salad with
    Chicken, 45
Chicken sausages
Butter Beans, Italian Sausage, and
    Chard, 53
Chickpeas, Barbecue-Spiced
    Roasted, 24
Chiles
Basil Halibut with Jalapeño Butter, 111
Chipotle-Cilantro Tilapia, 113
Farmer's Salad, 147
Fire-Roasted Tomato Salsa, 23
Fried Pickled Peppers with Ginger
    Aïoli, 12
Grilled Shrimp in Coconut Milk
    Sauce, 124
Picadillo Poppers, 13
Zesty Green Bean Slaw, 145
Chipotle-Cilantro Tilapia, 113
Chocolate
Banana Split Cake, 179
Gooey Chocolate-Caramel Cake, 177
Raspberry Fudge Pudding Cake, 174
Salted Peanut Butter and Chocolate
    Blondies, 185
Classic Nachos, 16
Coconut-Curry Noodle Bowl, 50
Confetti Corn Salad, 148
Corn
Basil Shrimp Chowder, 129
Brunswick Stew, 74
Confetti Corn Salad, 148
Farmer's Salad, 147
Harvest Succotash, 146
Mexican Corn-Chicken Casserole, 43
Spicy Skillet Pork Chops, 85
Tex-Mex Potato Salad, 149
Creamy Alfredo with Bacon and
    Peas, 97
Creamy Chicken Enchiladas, 30
Creamy Tuna-Noodle Toss, 120
Curried Chicken Salad, 39

D
Dates, Bacon-Filled Medjool, 19
Desserts. *See also* Bar cookies; Cakes
Bananas Foster Bake, 164
Blackberry-Blueberry Cobbler, 168
Grapefruit and Pear Crumble, 166
Green Apple-Chardonnay Granita, 173
Lemon Bar Ice Cream Sandwiches, 172
Peach-Cardamom Slab Pie, 171
Puffed Oven Pancake with Glazed
    Apples, 163
Raspberry Fudge Pudding Cake, 174
Stone Fruit-Coconut Crisp, 169
Drinks
Pink Rhubarb Lemonade, 26
Sangria, 27

E
Easy Hash Brown Bake, 152
Edamame
Harvest Succotash, 146
Spicy Asian Pork Cabbage Rolls, 90
Eggplant and Chicken Stuffed Shells, 6
Eggs
Egg Baguette Bake, 99
Sriracha Deviled Eggs, 18
Tex-Mex Potato Salad, 149
Espresso-Marinated Flank Steak, 70

F
Farmer's Salad, 147
Fennel
Chicken Paillard Salad, 31
Tilapia Pasta, 108
Fire-Roasted Tomato Salsa, 23
Fish and shellfish. *See also* Salmon;
    Shrimp; Tuna
Basil Halibut with Jalapeño Butter, 111
Chipotle-Cilantro Tilapia, 113
Parmesan-Crusted Cod with Garlicky
    Summer Squash, 110
Thai Coconut and Basmati Rice with
    Seared Scallops, 130
Tilapia Pasta, 108
French-Style Green Beans with Lemon
    and Walnuts, 144
Fresh Apple Snack Cake, 180
Fried Pickled Peppers with Ginger
    Aïoli, 12

G
Ginger-Soy Pork Chops on Greens, 84
Gooey Chocolate-Caramel Cake, 177
Grapefruit
Chicken Paillard Salad, 31
Grapefruit and Pear Crumble, 166
Greek Chicken and Pita Casserole, 46

Greek Chicken Kabobs, 48
Green Apple-Chardonnay Granita, 173
Green beans
Farmer's Salad, 147
French-Style Green Beans with Lemon
    and Walnuts, 144
Mini Meat Loaves with Potatoes and
    Beans, 81
Rosemary and Ravioli Chicken
    Soup, 56
Zesty Green Bean Slaw, 145
Greens. *See also* Arugula; Cabbage;
    Spinach
Butter Beans, Italian Sausage, and
    Chard, 53
Ginger-Soy Pork Chops on Greens, 84
Harvest Succotash, 146
Grilled dishes
Basil and Olive Potatoes, 155
Espresso-Marinated Flank Steak, 70
Fire-Roasted Tomato Salsa, 23
Ginger-Soy Pork Chops on Greens, 84
Grilled Shrimp in Coconut Milk
    Sauce, 124
Honey-Sriracha Grilled Chicken
    Thighs, 51
Picadillo Poppers, 13
Tarragon-Blue Cheese Turkey
    Patties, 67
Warm Brussels Sprouts Salad with
    Chicken, 45

H
Ham
Easy Hash Brown Bake, 152
Ham Balls in Barbecue Sauce, 9
Ham, Cheese, and Turkey
    Stromboli, 64
Roasted Pear-Ham Melts, 100
Harvest Succotash, 146
Honey-Sriracha Grilled Chicken Thighs, 51

I
Italian Roast Beef Slider Melts, 77
Italian Roasted Chicken and Vegetable
    Toss, 40

K
Korean Beef Lettuce Wraps, 11

L
Lemons
French-Style Green Beans with Lemon
    and Walnuts, 144
Lemon Bar Ice Cream Sandwiches, 172
Lemon-Herb Roasted Salmon with
    Broccoli and Tomatoes, 115
Lemony Tuna Salad, 121

Lima beans
Brunswick Stew, 74
Harvest Succotash, 146
Lime-Ginger Dressing, 128

M

Mangoes
Thai Coconut and Basmati Rice with
Seared Scallops, 130
Mexican Corn-Chicken Casserole, 43
Mexican Red Rice, 156
Mini Meat Loaves with Potatoes and
Beans, 81

Mushrooms
Bacon-Stuffed Mushrooms, 8
Chicken Marsala Skillet, 36
Italian Roasted Chicken and
Vegetable Toss, 40
Orange Teriyaki Beef Stew, 75
Pork and Wild Rice Soup, 105
Roasted Sausage with Mushrooms,
Squash, and Polenta, 93
Salmon and Cheese Stuffed
Mushrooms, 8
Spicy Asian Pork Cabbage Rolls, 90

N

Nacho Chicken Drummettes, 52

Nectarines
Stone Fruit-Coconut Crisp, 169

Noodles
Coconut-Curry Noodle Bowl, 50
Creamy Tuna-Noodle Toss, 120
Peanutty Noodle Slaw, 137
Spicy Shrimp with Cabbage-Noodle
Slaw, 127
Tuna-Noodle Casserole, 123

O

Oats
Bananas Foster Bake, 164
Grapefruit and Pear Crumble, 166
Stone Fruit-Coconut Crisp, 169

Oranges
Curried Chicken Salad, 39
Orange Teriyaki Beef Stew, 75
Roasted Radishes with Orange
Vinaigrette, 140
Shaved Brussels Sprouts with Green
Onion Vinaigrette, 138
Warm Brussels Sprouts Salad with
Chicken, 45
Overgrown Garden Turkey Melt, 65

P

Parmesan-Crusted Cod with Garlicky
Summer Squash, 110

Parsnips
Pork Chops with Roasted Vegetables
and Balsamic Drizzle, 82

Pasta. *See also* Noodles
Chicken and Eggplant Stuffed Shells, 6
Chicken Caesar Lasagna, 33
Creamy Alfredo with Bacon and
Peas, 97
Penne and Asparagus Salad, 136
Rosemary and Ravioli Chicken
Soup, 56
Salmon Vera Cruz, 114
Summer Spaghetti Salad, 135
Sweet Potato-Chorizo Lasagna, 95
Tacos in Pasta Shells, 78
Tilapia Pasta, 108

Peaches
Peach-Cardamom Slab Pie, 171
Stone Fruit-Coconut Crisp, 169

Peanut butter
Peanut Chicken Satay Stir-Fry, 44
Peanutty Noodle Slaw, 137
Salted Peanut Butter and Chocolate
Blondies, 185

Pears
Grapefruit and Pear Crumble, 166
Pear and Sweet Potato Soup, 157
Roasted Cabbage with Pears, 141
Roasted Pear-Ham Melts, 100

Peas
Creamy Alfredo with Bacon and
Peas, 97
Creamy Tuna-Noodle Toss, 120
Penne and Asparagus Salad, 136

Pepperoni
Pizza Dip, 22
Smoky Pizza Melts, 102
Zoodle Pizza Casserole, 96

Peppers. *See also* Chiles
Chicken Fajitas in a Flash, 38
Chicken Tortilla Soup, 59
Stuffed Fresh Sweet Peppers, 14
Picadillo Poppers, 13
Pie, Peach-Cardamom Slab, 171

Pineapple
Sweet-Spicy Barbecue Chicken
Sliders, 61
Pink Rhubarb Lemonade, 26
Pizza Dip, 22

Pizza dough
Buffalo Chicken Rolls, 62
Ham, Cheese, and Turkey
Stromboli, 64

Plums
Stone Fruit-Coconut Crisp, 169
Polenta, Roasted Sausage with
Mushrooms, Squash, and, 93

Pork. *See also* Bacon; Ham; Pork
sausages; Prosciutto
Brunswick Stew, 74
Ginger-Soy Pork Chops on Greens, 84
Ham Balls in Barbecue Sauce, 9
Pork and Potatoes with Minted
Yogurt, 87

Pork and Squash Enchiladas, 89
Pork and Wild Rice Soup, 105
Pork Cassoulet, 88
Pork Chops with Roasted Vegetables
and Balsamic Drizzle, 82
Spicy Asian Pork Cabbage Rolls, 90
Spicy Skillet Pork Chops, 85

Pork sausages
Baked Tomato-Mozzarella Spread, 21
Cajun Sausage-Potato Soup, 103
Egg Baguette Bake, 99
Roasted Sausage with Mushrooms,
Squash, and Polenta, 93
Sweet Potato-Chorizo Lasagna, 95
Pot Pie, Beef Stew, 73

Potatoes. *See also* Sweet potatoes
Baby Potatoes Roasted in Salt, 17
Basil and Olive Potatoes, 155
Brunswick Stew, 74
Cajun Sausage-Potato Soup, 103
Easy Hash Brown Bake, 152
Mini Meat Loaves with Potatoes and
Beans, 81
Pear and Sweet Potato Soup, 157
Pork and Potatoes with Minted
Yogurt, 87
Rosemary and Ravioli Chicken
Soup, 56
Tex-Mex Potato Salad, 149
Zucchini and Crispy Potato Salad, 151

Prosciutto
Penne and Asparagus Salad, 136
Prosciutto-Basil Cheese Balls, 20
Puffed Oven Pancake with Glazed
Apples, 163

R

Radishes with Orange Vinaigrette,
Roasted, 140
Raspberry Fudge Pudding Cake, 174
Rhubarb Lemonade, Pink, 26

Rice and wild rice
Baked Shrimp and Rice, 125
Mexican Corn-Chicken Casserole, 43
Mexican Red Rice, 156
Picadillo Poppers, 13
Pork and Wild Rice Soup, 105
Spicy Asian Pork Cabbage Rolls, 90
Thai Coconut and Basmati Rice with
Seared Scallops, 130
Roasted Cabbage with Pears, 141
Roasted Pear-Ham Melts, 100
Roasted Radishes with Orange
Vinaigrette, 140
Roasted Sausage with Mushrooms,
Squash, and Polenta, 93
Rosemary and Ravioli Chicken Soup, 56

S

Salad dressings
Lime-Ginger Dressing, 128

Salads
Basil and Olive Potatoes, 155
Chicken Paillard Salad, 31
Confetti Corn Salad, 148
Curried Chicken Salad, 39
Farmer's Salad, 147
Lemony Tuna Salad, 121
Peanutty Noodle Slaw, 137
Penne and Asparagus Salad, 136
Shaved Brussels Sprouts with Green
 Onion Vinaigrette, 138
Spicy Shrimp with Cabbage-Noodle
 Slaw, 127
Summer Spaghetti Salad, 135
Tex-Mex Potato Salad, 149
Warm Brussels Sprouts Salad with
 Chicken, 45
Zesty Green Bean Slaw, 145
Zucchini and Crispy Potato Salad, 151

Salmon
Lemon-Herb Roasted Salmon with
 Broccoli and Tomatoes, 115
Salmon and Cheese Stuffed
 Mushrooms, 8
Salmon Patties with Parsley and
 Mayo, 119
Salmon Vera Cruz, 114
Salmon with Roasted Tomatoes and
 Shallots, 118
Salmon with Tomatoes and Olives, 116
Salted Peanut Butter and Chocolate
 Blondies, 185

Sandwiches
Buffalo Chicken Rolls, 62
Italian Roast Beef Slider Melts, 77
Overgrown Garden Turkey Melt, 65
Roasted Pear-Ham Melts, 100
Smoky Pizza Melts, 102
Sweet-Spicy Barbecue Chicken
 Sliders, 61
Tarragon-Blue Cheese Turkey
 Patties, 67
Sangria, 27
Savory Double-Walnut Scones, 159
Scallops, Thai Coconut and Basmati
 Rice with Seared, 130
Shaved Brussels Sprouts with Green
 Onion Vinaigrette, 138

Shrimp
Baked Shrimp and Rice, 125
Basil Shrimp Chowder, 129
Grilled Shrimp in Coconut Milk
 Sauce, 124
Spicy Shrimp with Cabbage-Noodle
 Slaw, 127
Smoky Pizza Melts, 102

Soups. *See also* Stews
Basil Shrimp Chowder, 129
Cajun Sausage-Potato Soup, 103
Chicken Tortilla Soup, 59
Coconut-Curry Noodle Bowl, 50
Pear and Sweet Potato Soup, 157
Pork and Wild Rice Soup, 105
Rosemary and Ravioli Chicken
 Soup, 56
Spice-and-Honey Roasted Carrots, 143
Spicy Asian Pork Cabbage Rolls, 90
Spicy Shrimp with Cabbage-Noodle
 Slaw, 127
Spicy Skillet Pork Chops, 85

Spinach
Chicken Alfredo Cauliflower Rice
 Bake, 49
Chicken Paillard Salad, 31
Chicken and Spinach Phyllo Bake, 55
Chicken Caesar Lasagna, 33
Creamy Chicken Enchiladas, 30
Ham, Cheese, and Turkey
 Stromboli, 64
Overgrown Garden Turkey Melt, 65

Squash. *See also* Zucchini
Parmesan-Crusted Cod with Garlicky
 Summer Squash, 110
Pork and Squash Enchiladas, 89
Roasted Sausage with Mushrooms,
 Squash, and Polenta, 93
Summer Spaghetti Salad, 135
Sriracha Deviled Eggs, 18
Steak with Spicy Balsamic Glaze, 72

Stews
Beef Stew Pot Pie, 73
Brunswick Stew, 74
Orange Teriyaki Beef Stew, 75
Stone Fruit-Coconut Crisp, 169

Strawberries
Banana Split Cake, 179
Stromboli, Ham, Cheese, and Turkey, 64
Stuffed Fresh Sweet Peppers, 14
Summer Spaghetti Salad, 135

Sweet potatoes
Baked Curried Chicken with
 Cauliflower, 32
Pear and Sweet Potato Soup, 157
Pork Chops with Roasted Vegetables
 and Balsamic Drizzle, 82
Sweet Potato-Chorizo Lasagna, 95
Sweet-Spicy Barbecue Chicken
 Sliders, 61

T

Tacos in Pasta Shells, 78
Tangy Apricot-Rosemary Bars with Pine
 Nut Streusel, 183
Tarragon-Blue Cheese Turkey Patties, 67
Tex-Mex Potato Salad, 149
Thai Coconut and Basmati Rice with
 Seared Scallops, 130

Tilapia Pasta, 108

Tomatoes
Baked Tomato-Mozzarella Spread, 21
Farmer's Salad, 147
Fire-Roasted Tomato Salsa, 23
Greek Chicken Kabobs, 48
Grilled Shrimp in Coconut Milk
 Sauce, 124
Lemon-Herb Roasted Salmon with
 Broccoli and Tomatoes, 115
Lemony Tuna Salad, 121
Pork Cassoulet, 88
Salmon Vera Cruz, 114
Salmon with Roasted Tomatoes and
 Shallots, 118
Salmon with Tomatoes and Olives, 116
Summer Spaghetti Salad, 135
Zucchini and Crispy Potato Salad, 151

Tortillas
Chicken Fajitas in a Flash, 38
Chipotle-Cilantro Tilapia, 113
Creamy Chicken Enchiladas, 30
Pork and Squash Enchiladas, 89

Tuna
Creamy Tuna-Noodle Toss, 120
Lemony Tuna Salad, 121
Tuna-Noodle Casserole, 123

Turkey and turkey sausages
Greek Chicken and Pita Casserole, 46
Ham, Cheese, and Turkey
 Stromboli, 64
Overgrown Garden Turkey Melt, 6
Pork Cassoulet, 88
Tarragon-Blue Cheese Turkey
 Patties, 67

V

Vegetables. *See also* specific
 vegetables
Italian Roast Beef Slider Melts, 77
Peanut Chicken Satay Stir-Fry, 44
Pork Chops with Roasted Vegetables
 and Balsamic Drizzle, 82

W

Warm Brussels Sprouts Salad with
 Chicken, 45

Z

Zesty Green Bean Slaw, 145
Zoodle Pizza Casserole, 96

Zucchini
Greek Chicken and Pita Casserole, 46
Italian Roasted Chicken and
 Vegetable Toss, 40
Parmesan-Crusted Cod with Garlicky
 Summer Squash, 110
Summer Spaghetti Salad, 135
Zoodle Pizza Casserole, 96
Zucchini and Crispy Potato Salad, 151

Metric Information

PRODUCT DIFFERENCES

Most of the ingredients called for in the recipes in this book are available in most countries. However, some are known by different names. Here are some common American ingredients and their possible counterparts:

- Sugar (white) is granulated, fine granulated, or castor sugar.
- Powdered sugar is icing sugar.
- All-purpose flour is enriched bleached or unbleached white household flour. When self-rising flour is used in place of all-purpose flour in a recipe that calls for leavening, omit the leavening agent (baking soda or baking powder) and salt.
- Light-color corn syrup is golden syrup.
- Cornstarch is cornflour.
- Baking soda is bicarbonate of soda.
- Vanilla or vanilla extract is vanilla essence.
- Green, red, or yellow sweet peppers are capsicums or bell peppers.
- Golden raisins are sultanas.

VOLUME AND WEIGHT

The United States traditionally uses cup measures for liquid and solid ingredients. The chart (above right) shows the approximate imperial and metric equivalents. If you are accustomed to weighing solid ingredients, the following approximate equivalents will be helpful.

- 1 cup butter, castor sugar, or rice = 8 ounces = ½ pound = 250 grams
- 1 cup flour = 4 ounces = ¼ pound = 125 grams
- 1 cup icing sugar = 5 ounces = 150 grams
- Canadian and U.S. volume for a cup measure is 8 fluid ounces (237 ml), but the standard metric equivalent is 250 ml.
- 1 British imperial cup is 10 fluid ounces.
- In Australia, 1 tablespoon equals 20 ml, and there are 4 teaspoons in the Australian tablespoon.
- Spoon measures are used for small amounts of ingredients. Although the size of the tablespoon varies slightly in different countries, for practical purposes and for recipes in this book, a straight substitution is all that's necessary. Measurements made using cups or spoons always should be level unless stated otherwise.

COMMON WEIGHT RANGE REPLACEMENTS

Imperial / U.S.	Metric
½ ounce	15 g
1 ounce	25 g or 30 g
4 ounces (¼ pound)	115 g or 125 g
8 ounces (½ pound)	225 g or 250 g
16 ounces (1 pound)	450 g or 500 g
1¼ pounds	625 g
1½ pounds	750 g
2 pounds or 2¼ pounds	1,000 g or 1 Kg

OVEN TEMPERATURE EQUIVALENTS

Fahrenheit Setting	Celsius Setting	Gas Setting
300°F	150°C	Gas Mark 2 (very low)
325°F	160°C	Gas Mark 3 (low)
350°F	180°C	Gas Mark 4 (moderate)
375°F	190°C	Gas Mark 5 (moderate)
400°F	200°C	Gas Mark 6 (hot)
425°F	220°C	Gas Mark 7 (hot)
450°F	230°C	Gas Mark 8 (very hot)
475°F	240°C	Gas Mark 9 (very hot)
500°F	260°C	Gas Mark 10 (extremely hot)
Broil	Broil	Grill

*Electric and gas ovens may be calibrated using celsius. However, for an electric oven, increase celsius setting 10 to 20 degrees when cooking above 160°C. For convection or forced air ovens (gas or electric), lower the temperature setting 25°F/10°C when cooking at all heat levels.

BAKING PAN SIZES

Imperial / U.S.	Metric
9×1½-inch round cake pan	22- or 23×4-cm (1.5 L)
9×1½-inch pie plate	22- or 23×4-cm (1 L)
8×8×2-inch square cake pan	20×5-cm (2 L)
9×9×2-inch square cake pan	22- or 23×4.5-cm (2.5 L)
11×7×1½-inch baking pan	28×17×4-cm (2 L)
2-quart rectangular baking pan	30×19×4.5-cm (3 L)
13×9×2-inch baking pan	34×22×4.5-cm (3.5 L)
15×10×1-inch jelly roll pan	40×25×2-cm
9×5×3-inch loaf pan	23×13×8-cm (2 L)
2-quart casserole	2 L

U.S. / STANDARD METRIC EQUIVALENTS

⅛ teaspoon = 0.5 ml	
¼ teaspoon = 1 ml	
½ teaspoon = 2 ml	
1 teaspoon = 5 ml	
1 tablespoon = 15 ml	
2 tablespoons = 25 ml	
¼ cup = 2 fluid ounces = 50 ml	
⅓ cup = 3 fluid ounces = 75 ml	
½ cup = 4 fluid ounces = 125 ml	
⅔ cup = 5 fluid ounces = 150 ml	
¾ cup = 6 fluid ounces = 175 ml	
1 cup = 8 fluid ounces = 250 ml	
2 cups = 1 pint = 500 ml	
1 quart = 1 litre	